Aviva-No

Aviva-No

SHIMON ADAF

Translated from the Hebrew by YAEL SEGALOVITZ

Alice James Books
FARMINGTON, MAINE
alicejamesbooks.org

10 9 8 7 6 5 4 3 2 1

Alice James Books are published by Alice James Poetry Cooperative, Inc.,
an affiliate of the University of Maine at Farmington.

Alice James Books
114 Prescott Street
Farmington, ME 04938
www.alicejamesbooks.org

Library of Congress Cataloging-in-Publication Data

Names: Adaf, Shimon, author. | Segalovitz, Yael, translator. | Adaf, Shimon.
Aviva-no. English. | Adaf, Shimon, Aviva-no.
Title: Aviva-no / Shimon Adaf ; translated from Hebrew by Yael Segalovitz.
Description: Farmington, Maine : Alice James Books, 2019. | In English with
original Hebrew text.
Identifiers: LCCN 2019012545 (print) | LCCN 2019013012 (ebook) | ISBN
9781948579612 (eBook) | ISBN 9781948579056 (pbk. : alk. paper)
Classification: LCC PJ5055.2.D44 (ebook) | LCC PJ5055.2.D44 A9613 2019
(print) | DDC 892.41/7--dc23
LC record available at https://lccn.loc.gov/2019012545

Alice James Books gratefully acknowledges support from individual donors, private foundations, the University
of Maine at Farmington, the National Endowment for the Arts, and the Amazon Literary Partnership.

Supported by: Am Ha-Sefer, The Israeli Fund for Translation of Hebrew Books, The Cultural
Administration, Israel Ministry of Culture and Sport, and The Rabinovich Foundation for the Arts.

Originally published in Hebrew by Dvir, 2009, and published in this volume courtesy of Dvir and
in arrangement with The Institute for The Translation of Hebrew Literature.

Cover art: "Rosh Hanikra" by Erez Segalovitz

Contents

Clangs on the anvil of light

It was once already

This translation is dedicated with gratitude to
Robert Alter and Taylor Johnston

"How Will I Speak Her?": A Critical Introduction to Aviva-No *by Yael Segalovitz*

"Elegy presents every thing as lost and gone, or absent and future."
—SAMUEL TAYLOR COLERIDGE

My first encounter with *Aviva-No*—the third and most recent poetry collection of the acclaimed Israeli author, Shimon Adaf—was of a mystical, or better yet a ghostly, nature. In entering a bookstore in Tel Aviv, a new slim book on the display table immediately caught my eye. There was nothing conspicuous about it; in fact, its appearance was quite underwhelming—a black cover and on it, a sandy-brown rectangle surrounding a dark title: *Aviva-No*. But emanating from this gravestone-like cover, and from the pages behind it, were aching voices: Aviva is no longer; Aviva, a presence in negation; Aviva, I pray, don't. Indeed, as I quickly learned, *Aviva-No* is a haunting, strikingly beautiful elegy that gives no solace to its bewitched reader. It pains, mourns, refuses to fathom, and desperately tries to articulate via its rich and inventive Hebrew, the loss of Aviva, Adaf's older sister, and by extension "every thing" that is "lost and gone," in Coleridge's words above.

Seldom in the history of elegy do we find the sister to be the object of lament, the one whose absence renders everything at once "absent and future." When women figures do enter the genre, they commonly take the form of a nymph, a muse, or an abstract

1

metaphor (recall Wera Knoop in Rilke's *Sonnets to Orpheus*).[1] Yet in *Aviva-No*, it is the death of the flesh and blood Aviva ("Forty-three years old, you are the woman you will always be"), which brings the world into utter collapse: "the whole world has broken so, facing Aviva-no." Adaf not only spares Aviva the stereotypical role of the goddess of inspiration; he presents her as the very intellectual who introduced the speaker of *Aviva-No*, and perhaps the poet himself, to the world of letters and literary art—"And here you set me down, showed me / the books"—a role reserved in the patriarchal tradition for masculine father figures.

Alongside Aviva, Adaf's cycle of poems finds another protagonist, the Hebrew language itself. Adaf's speaker, with his blazing grief, melts the Hebrew down only to then remold it into previously unknown forms. It is thus that in poem 13, "light" in its radiation "*entifies* objects", and in poem 3, the ghosts of the dead are said to have "feared *at*" the speaker. In the same vein, the overbearing heat that arises from Adaf's poems allows him to fuse together Hebrew words from distant semantic realms in order to accomplish the impossible task of putting loss into words. The speaker's body is depicted, in the poem that opens the second section of the collection, as being *mushar*, "word by word". *Mushar* does not exist as a verb in Hebrew, but it grammatically makes sense to the reader as the passive participle of either the verb "to sing" (from the root sh.i.r) or of the verb "to cast off" (as in a tree shedding its leaves, from the root n.sh.r). This linguistic deformation works to conjure an emphatic image: the speaker's body appears as an entity that is slowly, "word by word," decomposing itself, while also triggering, precisely through this process of decay, the creation of "song," a term that in Hebrew refers both to poetry and to music.

Paradoxically, this linguistic flexibility, which the speaker finds in Hebrew, and which enables him to articulate Aviva's death, also sets off his rage against the language. He depicts Hebrew words, in poem 15, as "malicious sluts [who] say Aviva is gone" by lending themselves a vehicle for this dreadful news. By way of revenge, the speaker swears to "lay bare [the words'] roots, / their evil-doings I shall dash against the stone..." This line alludes to the horrible concluding image of Psalms 137. The psalm famously opens with the mourners—the Israelite captives, exiled from Jerusalem by the Babylonians—as they express their sorrow via song, very much like Adaf's speaker: "By the rivers of Babylon,

---

[1] Scholarship presents a complex picture of the role women play in the genre of elegy. On the one hand, articles such as Celeste M. Schenck's seminal "Feminism and Deconstruction: Re-Constructing the Elegy" emphasize the patriarchal thrust of the genre. She writes, "The funeral elegy is, from its inception in the poetry of Theocritus and his followers, Bion and Moschus, a resolutely patriarchal genre... it is modelled on archaic initiation rituals of [a] younger man by an elder" (*Tulsa Studies in Women's Literature* 5, no. 1 [1986], 13). On the other hand, critics such as Gail Holst-Warhaft trace women as makers and performers of lament to classical Greece (*Dangerous Voices: Women's Laments and Greek Literature* [London & New York: Routledge, 1992]). In *Aviva-No*, Adaf considers the two facets of the genre. As I will discuss below, he reacts against the patriarchal formula of elegy through the queering of gender and sex, and, in the spirit of Holst-Warhaft, evokes the ancient role of women as professional lamenters, specifically in the Middle Eastern tradition.

there we sat down, yea, we wept, when we remembered Zion" (KJV).[2] But Adaf points not to this opening melancholic image but to the violent one which brings the psalm to a close, depicting the Israelites' vengeful rage against their captives: "daughter of Babylon the despoiler, happy who pays you back in kind, for what you did to us. Happy who seizes and smashes your infants against the rock" (RA). In *Aviva-No*, rage is directed at Hebrew itself, the language that functions as the condition of possibility for the expression of the speaker's pain. That is, within the poetic universe of *Aviva-No*, Hebrew is the agent of both destruction and reconstruction. I will return to poem 15 below, but for now suffice it to say that this unique combination gives the collection its avant-garde form and allows it to mourn the dead while, in the same throbbing breath, renewing language.

Aviva-No's poignant expression of personal loss nevertheless makes an important intervention in a much larger Israeli cultural and political conversation that holds global relevance. This may very well be related to Adaf's own biography, which encapsulates and brings into stark relief the most intractable conflicts underlying Israeli identity politics today. Adaf is a son of Moroccan immigrants, who have historically been grouped in Israeli culture (together with immigrants from other North African and Middle Eastern communities) under the rubric of "Mizrachi" ("Eastern") Jews. The Mizrachi rebellion against their long-lasting, systematic exclusion from the Israeli cultural and political mainstream reached a fever pitch in the last decade, expressed, among other developments, by the establishment of an ambitious young coterie of poets—named "Ars-Poetica"—who raise the banner of the Mizrachi struggle in their work.[3] Adaf, for his part, takes a different stance within this struggle. Undoubtedly, his Moroccan upbringing and Mizrachi roots are strewn across *Aviva-No*. To mention just one example out of many, Adaf invokes the longstanding Middle-Eastern tradition, mentioned already in the Book of Jeremiah (9:17), of looking to women for the production and performance of lament, in an effort to unsettle the abovementioned elegiac patriarchal formula. For that reason, as early as the second poem, Adaf portrays three women, three sisters to be exact, as the ones who try to sew together the texture—and text—of Aviva's body, and her loss: "The remaining sisters sit and sew / the shreds of the rent body." But Adaf's identification with and reliance on Mizrachi Middle-Eastern tradition never takes the form of an explicit and generalized statement, neither in *Aviva-No* nor in the other works that comprise his oeuvre. In his mind, the resistance to naming—to raising any banner whatsoever—is itself a political move, a possible reason for his reluctance to publicly align himself with

---

[2] I have used throughout either the King James or Robert Alter's translation of the Bible, here marked as KJV and RA, respectively.
[3] The group's name is a wordplay in Hebrew, alluding to Horace's *The Art of Poetry* while also reappropriating the derogatory term "ars", "pimp" in Arabic, which in the Israeli context is stereotypically associated with Mizrachi men. Important to note that Ars Poetica did not yet exist when *Aviva-No* was written, thus that Adaf's dialogue in this collection is with Ars Poetica's influential (yet too frequently unmentioned) precursors, such as Sami Shalom Chetrit, Mois Benarroch, Vicki Shiran, and Shelley Elkayam.

"Ars-Poetica." As he writes in his recent essay, "The I Who Desires to Declare I":[4]

> Once and again I pause in front of trees, the light arrested in their branches during certain hours of the day, in certain seasons. At times, other sights demand my presence, demand that I attend. A bird cutting through the air, the movement of shade, a countenance, a bodily gesture, eyes, the accent of people I loved which embodies endless warmth, customs and manners that form my very neural network, the cells that shape my veins… Even "Moroccanness" is too general a term for this claim made upon me… even "My Moroccanness" is an empty vessel. This claim has no name but the singular one I give it each time anew.[5]

There is no point, then, in searching for an overt invocation of Adaf's Mizrachi identity in *Aviva-No*. Instead, the contours of his singular experience of being in the world—structured by, yet surpassing the label "Moroccanness"—lie among the bougainvillea, almond trees, loam sandstones, hibiscus bushes, balsam trees, warblers, flame trees, crows, or asphalt lines that pave the imagined though profoundly Israeli landscape of *Aviva-No*.[6]

Adaf also conveys his Mizrachi background in *Aviva-No* via his ongoing dialogue with traditional Jewish texts and praxes. In the Israeli context, Mizrachi culture is historically associated with an intimate affinity for Jewish tradition that is not restricted to and by Jewish Law (a religious stance usually referred to as *masorti'ut*). Adaf was raised in an orthodox household, where, though his mother and father adhered to very different conceptions of the Jewish faith, they both encouraged him to acquire an in-depth Jewish education. His father especially hoped for him to become a rabbi and provided him with the required rigorous education. Adaf ended up veering away from this path, yet his multilingual knowledge of the Jewish sources reverberates throughout his work, from the Hebrew Bible, through the Aramaic Mishna and Talmud, all the way to the Jewish prayer book (this is especially true of Adaf's trilogy *Nuntia* [2010], *Mox Nox* [2011], and *De Urbibus Infenis* [2012]). In *Aviva-No* specifically, Adaf enters into dialogue with Jewish tradition through his repeated, and furious, addresses to God. Adaf's speaker does not denounce God for the calamity that befell his family. Instead, in the spirit of Job or Jonah, he directs his fury at God, as in poem 7: "What were your words / to my sister / in the bathroom [...] He who sticks His blazing wrath / into mortal affairs, / with Your barren

---

[4] Shimon Adaf, "The I Who Desires to Declare I", in *I am Others* (Be'er Sheva: Kinneret, Zmora-Bitan, Dvir & Heksherim Institute, 2018), 9-19. All unattributed translations are mine.

[5] Ibid., 14.

[6] For an interesting exploration of Adaf's interaction with Mizrachi culture via multicultural poetic language, see Dorit Lemberger, "Questioning Boundaries of Language and the World: Ambivalence and Disillusionment in the Writings of Shimon Adaf," *Hebrew Studies* 56, no. 1 (2015): 265-294.

silence, in this morning / of unbearable pain, / You, / tell me –." In the following poem, number 8, Adaf's speaker forcefully accuses God of taking pleasure in death and in the unique form of address to the divine it elicits: "who else has praised thee thus / [...] with a sister, with her fleeting breath in the bathroom, with a / conquered heart and with flesh lying on the floor, turning blue, / bursting with a splendor of eternal silence, with a mother desperately kissing it / Who had once lauded thee." At the same time, Adaf remains critical of institutionalized religion, portraying, for instance, a rabbi who explains away Aviva's death with the simplistic theological argument: "a guardian angel [...] She is saving a foreign cousin / from being impaled on an iron pole." In the same vein, he also sarcastically depicts a "wise man" who enters the mourners' house and "orders": "donate to / the synagogue."

However, what is most striking in Adaf's engagement with the Jewish sources in *Aviva-No* is his frequent gestures toward Jewish mourning rituals, particularly esoteric ones, whose significance is for the most part lost on its practitioners. These idiosyncratic practices permit *Aviva-No* to communicate the mourners' collapse of sensemaking in the face of loss. Such, for instance, is the ritual of reading during the *shiv'ah* (the seven days of mourning) the Mishnaic text "Stoking the Incense" (*pitum ha-ketoret*), which details the 365 ingredients that were required to light the incense offering in the Holy Temple of Jerusalem. "Pitum ha-ketoret" reads like a secret recipe, containing names of ingredients whose meaning has been lost over time, and meticulously regulating a ritual that has long disappeared from existence.[7] This enigmatic text, which some even believe holds mystical powers, makes its entrance already in *Aviva-No*'s first poem, which concludes: "and the heart is arrested and named mere breath / for the three hundred and sixty five minas of smoke within it / against the count of three hundred and sixty five days of." This final line lingers on the tongue in its uncanny unconcluded form ("days *of*"), mimicking the abrupt cessation of Aviva's life. Yet by gesturing towards this Mishnaic portion, Adaf also highlights the Jewish ritual's role—precisely due to its unintelligibility—in helping the mourner to cope with a time out of joint, and engage in the labor of sewing the 365 days of the year back together, even if this labor is doomed to fail. After all, the fictional time depicted in the collection is spread over one year exactly (the Jewish year of mourning), opening and closing with the Hebrew month of *Kislev* in which the death took place, and in between following the months of the Jewish calendar ("*Shevat* crept in coils of ice," "*Adar* unfolds in melded skies," "the heavy heat of *Tammuz*," "[a] broiling *Av*").

For Haviva Pedaya, a prominent Mizrachi Israeli poet and scholar, Adaf's engagement with esoteric Jewish texts has a strong political valence. In referring to Adaf's

---

[7] *Pitum ha-ketoret* is said by the practicing Jew several times a day, every day. However, it receives special status during the *shiv'ah*, when it is read in the mourners' house.

intertextual dialogue with *"pitum ha-ketoret,"* she writes:

> In the context of Israeli culture, a Mizrachi child frequently finds himself laboring to comprehend the full meaning of a cultural object, which perhaps captivates him with its beauty, but also pushes him away since he lacks the tools needed to decode it. Why shouldn't the center stand thus facing the periphery [...] and labor to understand its opaqueness? What is peripheral here [in *Aviva-No*], you ask? The endlessly layered language that was submerged [in Israel] under one flattened Hebrew.[8]

Pedaya configures together cultural and geographical exclusion. She links the cultural peripheralization of the "endlessly layered" Hebrew that Mizrachi tradition preserves in its unique affinity for Jewish tradition, with the geographic peripheralization of Mizrachi Jews (The "periphery" is colloquial Hebrew for the predominantly Mizrachi under-privileged areas, especially in the south of the country). And indeed, *Aviva-No* takes place in the Israeli geo-cultural outskirts, more specifically, in the terror-stricken Gaza-bordering city of Sderot, where Adaf grew up, and where his speaker bemoans Aviva.

As the target of dozens of rockets since the second Palestinian intifada (September 2000), Sderot has become one of the most prevalent symbols in the Israeli imaginary for the devastating Israeli-Palestinian conflict. It is not surprising, then, to find that "Qassam rockets," "bomb shelters," and the "Gaza Strip" recur throughout *Aviva-No*. Yet here as well, Adaf refuses to fight any one-sided battle. He will not emphasize the suffering on one side of the border at the expense of the other. As he writes in poem 32, "So where is the gate / in Gaza, in Sderot – // The underworld of former times; the air / still faint / and we go through." The "underworld" in *Aviva-No* extends its hellish existence over the two sides of the border, a territory scorched by political forces blind to human misery "in Gaza, in Sderot." Within this earthly inferno, even natural beauty is out of reach: "Orchid, a tree, perhaps / only a bush, and still, a verdant vessel / seizing voices that *Nissan* / threatens to eject: a stamen – a caw of color, a petal – / a howl of hue. / This is all in reach, that is, / unreachable, in Gaza, in Sderot, / an enthralled *Adar* is swarming" (poem 41). In the same vein, Adaf insists throughout the collection on bringing to the fore the frequently silenced presence of Arabic in the Hebrew language, in Jewish history, and in the mouths of Palestinians and Arab-Israelis within the Israeli public sphere. Adaf compels his reader to recall both the intimate link between Mizrachi and Arab cultures, and the long-standing historical dialogue between Jewish and Arabic-speaking communities and literatures. In poem 25, for example, he writes: "and the neighbor

---

[8] Haviva Pedaya, "*Aviva-No* by Shimon Adaf: Not by Way of Verse but by Pain" ["אביבה-לא מאת שמעון אדף: לא על דרך השירה אלא פדא: וזעמש תאמ אל-הביבא"], *Ha'aretz*, March 24, 2010. https://www.haaretz.co.il/literature/poetry/1.1194518.

rants unaware in Arabic / *Wu'natalti ruha u'shmait batrai kal zia sagi* –". In this line, Adaf deftly mobilizes the orthographic similarity between the Hebrew term for Arabic (*Aravit*) and the name of the Jewish evening prayer service (*Arvit*), making the neighbor rant "in Arabic" Aramaic words from the Jewish prayer "And a Redeemer Shall Come to Zion".[9] In this way, Adaf underscores the close affinity between Arab and Jewish traditions. Even more provocatively, through this linguistic manipulation, he is able to lure the reader, especially the secular one unacquainted with the Jewish prayer book, into believing that the neighbor's Aramaic prayer *is* indeed a "rant" in Arabic, thus revealing how Aramaic and Arabic are similarly foreign to the contemporary ear. All this is astutely done without ceasing to summon Aviva. After all, the sentence Adaf quotes from "And a Redeemer Shall Come to Zion" conjures precisely the figure of the ghost: "then a spirit [also, ghost] carried me away, and behind me I heard a great roaring sound".

Adaf, then, has a foot in both *Mizrachi* and *Ashkenazi* (stereotypically construed as "Eastern" and "Western") identities, religious and secular thought, and, to a certain degree, Jewish and Arab cultures, the three binaries that set the parameters of contemporary Israeli socio-political discourse. Adaf adamantly resists adhering to any stable identity on these three continuums, since, as he further writes in "The I Who Desires to Declare I": "In our times, the field of representations is replete with invitations to… endlessly speak out one's identity, to make it easily distinguishable from the other endless array of possibilities presented to the individual, so that one could stop and say: I'm an A and a B and a C, with a bit of D on the side."[10] The result, he warns, is that

> self-definition [is] achieved through constant identification with a certain identity category. Consequently, all internal efforts are directed at consolidating that identity category, sealing its cracks and fissures, differentiating it from other [identity] categories, which are then perceived, as a result of the effort to entrench oneself in one's category, as hostile. Thus, the core of identity politics as it is practiced in everyday discourse is sameness and not otherness, a desire towards identification.[11]

At the heart of *Aviva-No* is a subjectivity that teeters on the edge of the abyss, of utter collapse in the face of loss ("I ceased to see / how I shall live / life anymore / what of"). This driving disintegrating force makes Adaf's continuous battle against "sameness" even more pronounced in this work than in his oeuvre more generally. As I've observed, Adaf resists any easy "identification" in *Aviva-No* by unsettling the narrow, stable categories through

---

[9] "And a Redeemer Shall Come to Zion" is said during the evening prayer (*Aravit*) on Saturdays and during special occasions such as the fast day of *Tisha B'Av*, and the holiday of *Purim*.
[10] Adaf, "The I Who Desires to Say I," 9.
[11] Ibid., 12.

which his poetry is in danger of being understood when read against the backdrop of his biography. He also consistently, systematically, and ingeniously defamiliarizes Hebrew through his elegiac poetry, making it foreign even, and perhaps especially, to its native speakers. Yet, as one would expect from a poet dedicated to otherness, Adaf takes another, unexpected route in destabilizing a consolidated identity. He does this by queering both gender and sex, placing his speaker, his reader, and even Hebrew itself in an imaginary body that refuses the confines of the imposed rigid categories masculine vs. feminine, man vs. woman.

As we recall, in poem 15, Adaf compares Hebrew words to "sluts" (whose babies the enraged speaker craves to "dash against the stones") in the spirit of the biblical revenge against the Babylonians. This poem, then, begins by presenting Hebrew as a woman in an overdetermined fashion; it does so in metaphorical figuration ("slut," mother), through its intertextual dialogue (Hebrew is the equivalent of the "daughter of Babylon the despoiler"), and by highlighting grammatical gender as a sight of personification ("language" is grammatically feminine in Hebrew).[12] In this way, the readers are led to infer that the speaker who refers to Hebrew as a "slut" and evokes the biblical misogynist scene (in which the Israelite male captives imagine punishing the Babylonian daughters for their fathers' violence) is a man. But the poem's second half subverts and unsettles its own established gender hierarchy. The speaker states "malicious sluts say Aviva is gone. / But I was / as well, Hebrew pounding on / my throat-bell, I answered aye. / It has the dick of a camel, that one." We learn that the ostensibly male speaker of the poem, who invoked the "malicious sluts," confesses "I was, as well," leaving us to wonder: Is s/he a slut too? This question is dragged over to the next line, where a sexualized image presents Hebrew, supposedly a metaphorical woman, as the one doing the "pounding" with the speaker, who voluntarily participates ("I answered aye"). In this way, the simple binaries of passive/active and penetrating/penetrated are profoundly destabilized. This deconstruction reaches a crescendo in the final line, where Adaf's gender-sex provocation is necessarily lost in translation. The original Hebrew reads: "*She* has the dick of a camel, that one". The "she" in the original refers to the grammatically feminine Hebrew language, in this way foregrounding the question of gender and sex. Adaf leverages the fact that Hebrew is an exceedingly gendered language in order to boldly flaunt its intersexed figuration. Put bluntly, Adaf's Hebrew is a "she" with a "dick," and his male mourner is a "slut" being "pounded." In Adaf's universe, then, the very body of language evades "sameness," allowing him to impart fluidity to formal structures and identity categories.

---

[12] In this sense, Adaf participates in this poem in the destabilization of the pivotal metaphor of the land/city as a woman, which runs like a thread through Hebrew literature from the Bible to the present. This metaphorical system with its literary and political implications is the subject of Chana Kronfeld's book project, *The Land as Woman: The Afterlife of a Poetic Metaphor in Women's Modern Hebrew Poetry* (in preparation).

To come full circle, the effort of translating *Aviva-No* entailed a prolonged listening to and lingering with the collection's singular, haunting, poetic voices. However, like any ghostly utterance, these voices turned out to be difficult, if not impossible, to grasp and make legible in English; this was the case especially since, in contrast with Hebrew, English does not gender nouns, a trait of which Adaf makes extensive and crafty use. Moreover, Adaf's intense dialogue with Jewish sources and his multilingual play do not allow for an easy transition into a different linguistic realm. This is particularly felt in poem 28, where Adaf transcribes English in Hebrew letters, mimicking the Hebrew speaker's accent and common mistakes in what is considered in Israel the language of prestige. What I nevertheless labored to preserve at any cost was the emotional intensity of Adaf's experimental poetry, by resisting the temptation to smooth over *Aviva-No*'s unique and defamiliarizing texture, syntax, and structure. *Aviva-No* is a seismographic text, charting in its vibrating language the tectonic, transformative pain that erupts and consumes one's being in the face of death. My hope is that the readers of this translation will be able to feel these seismic waves pulsating under Adaf's words.

— Yael Segalovitz, May 2019

Whose time is it
like metal, retaining cold
and lightning.

And why should I live it,
weighing on the chest
any attempt to escape
will rupture the aorta.

(Object, 1)

שֶׁל מִי הַזְּמַן הַזֶּה
כְּמוֹ מַתָּכוֹת, צוֹבֵר הַקֹּר
וְהַבְּרָקִים.

וְלָמָּה שֶׁאֶחְיֶה אוֹתוֹ,
מֻנָּח עַל הֶחָזֶה
כָּל נִסָּיוֹן מִלּוֹט
יִקְרַע אֶת אַב הָעוֹרְקִים.

(דָּבָר, 1)

1.

I'm in a state of how does it go and I shall call it Aviva-no I shall call it sisterless

and I shall speak of it with straightforwardness not by way of verse but by pain

and thus is its Law it has no Law—stifling-breath angels and blazing-eyed

beasts, in the internet above and the buried books below, it has no

Law, it is only the moment piercing space like a pin into glass

and the heart is arrested and named mere breath

for the three hundred and sixty-five minas of smoke within it

against the count of three hundred and sixty-five days of.

א.

אֲנִי בְּמַצָּב אֵיךְ לְהַגְדִּירוֹ וְאֶקְרָאֵהוּ אֲבִיבָה-לֹא אֶקְרָאֵהוּ אֵינָחוֹת
וַאֲדַבְּרָה בּוֹ יְשִׁירוּת לֹא עַל דֶּרֶךְ הַשִּׁירָה אֶלָּא לְפִי כְּאֵב
וְזֹאת הִיא תּוֹרָתוֹ אֵין לוֹ תּוֹרָה – מַלְאָכִים מְחַנְּקִים נְשִׁימָה וְחַיּוֹת
בּוֹעֲרוֹת עֵינַיִם, בָּאִינְטֶרְנֶט מִמַּעַל וּבַסְּפָרִים הַנִּקְבָּרִים, אֵין
לוֹ תּוֹרָה, רַק הָרֶגַע בְּעַצְמוֹת הֶחָלָל הוּא נוֹקֵב כְּסַכָּה בִּזְכוּכִית
וְהַלֵּב הֶחָדוּל וְקָרוּי הֶבֶל
מִשּׁוּם שָׁלוֹשׁ מֵאוֹת שִׁשִּׁים וַחֲמִשָּׁה מָנִים שֶׁל עָשָׁן שֶׁבּוֹ
כְּנֶגֶד שָׁלוֹשׁ מֵאוֹת שִׁשִּׁים וַחֲמִשָּׁה מִנְיַן יְמוֹת.

2.

At night the destroyers are given permission,
the flaming vault of heavens, merciless. Downcast *Kislev*,
a black conflagration is within him.

The remaining sisters sit and sew
the shreds of the rent body.
One threads a string, the other
strikes the needle,
the third screams, oh no!
the finger, it is pricked.

Blinders of the moons, a sketch in silver
fine as cracked skin, and the fire
of the crimson drop is glowing.

Blood moves in the world yet suffices not for one being
to be saved
and blood spills, how to put it,
fountains and depths spring out
of valleys and hills.

ב.
_____

לַיְלָה רָשׁוּת לַמְחַבְּלִים הוּא,
לַהַט רְקִיעִים עָרֵל. כְּסִלֵּו הַסָּר יֵשׁ
לוֹ תַּבְעֵרָה שְׁחֹרָה.

יוֹשְׁבוֹת וּמַטְלִיאוֹת הָאַחֲיוֹת הַנּוֹתָרוֹת
מְקוֹם קְרִיעַת הַגּוּף.
אַחַת מַשְׁחֶלֶת חוּט, שְׁנִיָּה
מַכָּה בַּמַּחַט,
שְׁלִישִׁית צוֹוַחַת: אָח,
הָאֶצְבַּע, הִיא דְּקָרָה.

סַךְ הַסְּהָרִים שִׂרְטוּט שֶׁל כֶּסֶף
דַּק כְּמוֹ עוֹר נִבְקַע וְאֵשׁ
הָאַרְגָּמָן שֶׁל הַטִּפָּה זוֹרַחַת.

דָּם זָז בָּעוֹלָם וְלֹא מַסְפִּיק לְנֶפֶשׁ
אֵין דַּי לְהַצִּיל
וְדָם זָז, אֵיךְ לוֹמַר,
תְּהוֹם וַעֲיָנוֹת יוֹצְאִים
בָּעֵמֶק וּבָהָר.

3.

They all saw the signs and did not say,
but my mother spoke of her vision
a week before: deceased family
gather at the door,
trudge to the bedroom, ghostly faces
mourn with her. As for me, all those I invented
came back from the dead. On the sea shore
they feared at me, in the poisoned glare
of heavens' vault against electric light, in roiled
curtains near an oleander thicket, in a flock of nightingales,
in the halls, in soul-corrupting blogs.

Later, dreams, and not mine:
Light, rare, washing the living room,
a stranger in jeans and a T-shirt unbinds
my sister's throat. A guardian angel, explains the Rabbi.
She is saving a foreign cousin
from being impaled on an iron pole. Donate to
the synagogue, another wise man orders. Leaving,
a bag on her back, if only she
commanded, you go to your lives, we

ג.

לְכֻלָּם הָיוּ אוֹתוֹתֵיהֶם שָׁלֵם וְלֹא אָמְרוּ
אֲבָל אִמִּי סִפְּרָה אֵיךְ רָאֲתָה
שָׁבוּעַ קֹדֶם: בְּנֵי מִשְׁפַּחְתָּהּ
הַמָּנוּחִים נֶאֱסָפִים לַדֶּלֶת
וּמִשְׁתָּרְכִים לְחֶדֶר הַשֵּׁנָה, פְּנֵי רְפָאִים
נָדִים לָהּ. אֲנִי כָּל מִי שֶׁבָּדִיתִי
חָזַר מִן הַמֵּתִים. עַל חוֹף הַיָּם
הָיָה פַחְדָּם אֵלַי, בַּבֹהַק הַמֻּרְעָל שֶׁל
רְקִיעִים כְּנֶגֶד תְּאוּרַת חַשְׁמַל, בְּוִילָאוֹת
סוֹעִים סָמוּךְ לְסָבֶךְ הַהֲדוּף, בִּלְהַק זְמִירִים,
בַּפְּרוֹזְדוֹרִים, בַּבְּלוֹגִים מַדִּיחֵי הַנֶּפֶשׁ.

אַחַר כָּךְ חֲלוֹמוֹת, וְלֹא שֶׁלִּי:
אוֹר־אֵין־בִּלְתּוֹ שׁוֹטֵף אֶת הַסָּלוֹן,
גֶּבֶר זָר בְּגִ'ינְס וּבְטְרִיקוֹ מַתִּיר גְּרוֹנָה
שֶׁל אֲחוֹתִי. מַלְאָךְ שׁוֹמֵר, מַבְהִיר הָרַב.
הִיא מַצִּילָה בַּת דּוֹדָה רְחוֹקָה
מֵהִשְׁתַּפְּדוּת עַל מוֹט בַּרְזֶל. לִתְרֹם לְבֵית
הַכְּנֶסֶת, פּוֹקֵד חָכָם אַחֵר. יוֹצֵאת
תִּיק עַל גַּבָּהּ, לוּ רַק
הוֹרְתָה, אַתֶּם לְכוּ לְחַיֵּיכֶם, הָיִינוּ

would understand, but she

implores, I am not happy here, let go.

Our hands are stained, we stare at them all morning.

We did not ask for much, exposed to secrets –

in this hollowness to sort out voices, faces,

when hazy light burns over trees, in parlors of

wind, and suicidal rain between the larks in cyber chatter;

It is a sin to thus whet hours into beauty,

to mold from mounting pulse

an entity that precedes it.

No, presence without end, a fleet of wounds

nearing the annulment of all limits.

מְבִינִים אֶת הַדְּבָרִים, אֲבָל הִיא
מַפְצִיַרָה, לֹא טוֹב לִי פֹּה, הַרְפּוּ.

יָדֵינוּ עֲקֻבּוֹת, אָנוּ מַבִּיטִים בָּן כָּל הַבֹּקֶר.
מָה כְּבָר בִּקַּשְׁנוּ, מִגְלִים אֶל רְמָזִים –
בַּחֲלָלוּת הַזֹּאת לָבֹר קוֹלוֹת, פָּנִים
כְּשֶׁאוֹר אָבִיךְ דּוֹלֵק מֵעַל עֵצִים, בְּטַרְקְלִינִים שֶׁל
רוּחַ, וְגֶשֶׁם מִתְאַבֵּד בֵּין עֲפְרוֹנִים בְּסִיבֵּר הַבַּרְבֶּרֶת;
עָווֹן כָּךְ לְהַשְׁחִיז שָׁעוֹת לִיפִי,
לָצוּר מֵחֹלֶם מַחֲרִיף
יֶשְׁנוּת שֶׁהִיא רֵאשִׁית לוֹ.
לֹא, נוֹכְחוּת עַד תֹּם, עַד אֶפֶס גְּבוּלוֹתָיו
מַטָּס שֶׁל שְׂסוּפִים.

4.

I needed the body as well

to break

but it did not

crash

flocks of birds entered

the flesh

sparrows and bleeding wrens

sap seeping out of balsam trees

frozen as glass, shining

as a plastic scarf

under a moon thrown in the trash

I ceased to see

how I shall live

life anymore

what of

ד.

נִזְקַקְתִּי גַּם לַגּוּף

שֶׁיִּשָּׁבֵר

וְלֹא

נִשְׁבַּר

בָּאוּ סִיעוֹת צִפּוֹרִים

בַּבָּשָׂר

אַנְקוֹרִים חֲשׁוּיִים בְּדָמִים דְּרוּרִים

שְׂרָף נָטַף מֵעֲצֵי קָטָף

קְפוּאִים כְּמוֹ זְכוּכִית, זוֹרְחִים

כִּרְדִיד נַיְלוֹן

תַּחַת יָרֵחַ מְשֻׁלָּךְ בָּאַשְׁפָּה

חָדַלְתִּי מֵרְאוֹת

אֵיךְ אֶחְיֶה

בַּחַיִּים עוֹד

מִמָּה

5.

And I did not know that I would have to live

your death, and how easily

it would fit into words. Just as mother

explained to the grandchildren, we will

never see Aviva again. And I heard

her cry, not that howling

lamentation, just the flow

of one whose strength vanished in the flame.

And they asked, caught up in wondering,

if you climbed up to a star, what

would you do if it fell, would you be hungry.

And she put them in the bomb

shelter and came sobbing to

the living room where I sat

and said

how simple it is to see

in the dark, like an ember glowing wild—

losing a child means always losing a child.

ה.

וְלֹא יָדַעְתִּי שֶׁאֶצְטָרֵךְ לִחְיוֹת
אֶת מוֹתֵךְ, וְכַמָּה פָּשׁוּט יִהְיֶה לְנַסֵּחַ
אֶת זֶה. כְּמוֹ שֶׁאִמָּא
הַסְּבִירָה לַנְּכָדִים, לֹא נִרְאֶה
אֶת אֲבִיבָה עוֹד אַף פַּעַם. וְשָׁמַעְתִּי
אוֹתָהּ בּוֹכָה, לֹא הַקִּינָה
הַזֹּאת הַמְנַחֶמֶת, רַק הַשֶּׁטֶף
שֶׁל מִי שֶׁכּוֹחוֹתָיו אָפְסוּ בַּלֶּהָבָה.
וְהֵם שָׁאֲלוּ תְּפוּסֵי תְּמִיהָה
אִם טִפַּסְתְּ לַכּוֹכָב, מָה
תַּעֲשִׂי אִם יִפֹּל, אִם תִּהְיִי רְעֵבָה.
וְהִיא הִנִּיחָה אוֹתָם בְּמִסְתּוֹר
הַקָּסָאם וּבָאָה יְפוּחָה אֶל
הַסָּלוֹן שָׁם יָשַׁבְתִּי
וּכְבָר אָמַרְתִּי
כַּמָּה פָּשׁוּט לִרְאוֹת אֶת זֶה
בַּחֲשֵׁכָה כְּמוֹ גַחֶלֶת –
לְאַבֵּד יֶלֶד פֵּרוּשׁוֹ תָּמִיד לְאַבֵּד יֶלֶד.

6.

She had a heart heavier than the ocean

my mother

and it sank.

Do you feel the desert in your bones?

The sunken ships, stuck

like crosses in the sand, the wells empty

of stars, the pulse of the manna hailing down

do you recall?

הָיָה לָהּ לֵב כָּבֵד מִן הָאוֹקְיָנוֹס

לְאִמִּי

וְהוּא שָׁקַע.

אַתֶּם חָשִׁים בְּעַצְמוֹת אֶת הַמִּדְבָּר?

אֶת הַסְּפִינוֹת טְבוּעוֹת, תְּקוּעוֹת

בַּחוֹל כְּמוֹ צְלָבִים, אֶת הַבּוֹרוֹת רֵיקִים

מִכּוֹכָבִים, אֶת דֹּפֶק בְּרַד הַמָּן

אַתֶּם זוֹכְרִים?

7.

What were your words

to my sister

in the bathroom, on the

toilet

before

she turned her head to the wall.

Her arms' heft

ripped toilet paper

holder

from its place,

two hand towels

laid out at her feet.

He who sticks His blazing wrath

into mortal affairs,

with Your barren silence, in this morning

of unbearable pain,

You,

tell me—

‫ז.‬

‫מַה הָיָה דְּבָרֵךְ‬
‫אֶל אֲחוֹתִי‬
‫בַּשֵּׁרוּתִים, עַל‬
‫הָאַסְלָה‬
‫עַד‬
‫שֶׁהֵסַבָּה רֹאשׁ לַקִּיר.‬

‫הַכֹּבֶד שֶׁל זְרוֹעָה‬
‫נִתֵּק מִתְלֶה‬
‫נְיַר טוֹאָלֶט‬
‫מִמְּקוֹמוֹ,‬
‫שְׁתֵּי מַגְּבוֹת פָּנִים‬
‫יָשְׁרוּ מַרְגְּלוֹתֶיהָ.‬

‫הַתּוֹחֵב חֲרוֹן אַפּוֹ‬
‫לְעִסְקֵיהֶם שֶׁל בְּנֵי תְּמוּתָה,‬
‫בַּשֶּׁקֶט הַמַּחֲרִישׁ שֶׁלְּךָ, בְּבֹקֶר זֶה‬
‫שֶׁל חַלְחָלָה,‬
‫אָמַר לִי גַּם‬
‫אַתָּה –‬

27

8.

With what else should I praise thee, Lord, when I have praised with a rose's tap, with a cascade

of nightingales at dusk, with treetops trimmed by skies of tin, wrought from light, with the lightning's

strain dissolving the horizon, on the internet, *Hallel*,

in those hallucinatory depths Your apparition ascends, on the phone's display I praised thee, with a

text message: *call me now*,

and I praised thee with my brother's answer, with his city-splitting howl, boring through the ear:

You have to come. Aviva, Aviva is dead.

And I praised thee, I praised,

packing my clothes, thrust into lucidity, my legs quivering, *Hallel* at the gates of

the pathology clinic, *Hallel* Abu Kabir, in the oleander hedge I praised,

to its shelter my two brothers and I retreat to fall apart, and with the death certificate

I praised, *Hallel* was always on my lips, driving behind the ambulance

transporting her home, I praised all the way, an unclaimed winter, a clear winter, a winter

bursting bliss, *Hallel* at Nitzanim junction, in the traffic jam I praised, sitting

listening to the thaw's whisper, the ice melting in the container where her body,

autopsy-less, toxic-pure, regathers

its softness.

Thy seraphim

command them to ask

who else has praised thee thus

ח.

בַּמֶּה עוֹד לְהַלְלֵךְ וְהִלַּלְתִּיךְ בִּנְקִישַׁת הַוֶּרֶד, בְּמַפַּל זְמִירִים עִם עֶרֶב, בְּצַמָּרוֹת
בְּדוֹלְוֹת מִשְׁמֵי בְדִיל, קְנוּיוֹת מָאוֹר, בְּמֶתַח הַבָּרָק
הַמֻּפְרָק בָּאֹפֶק, עַל בָּמוֹת הָאִינְטֶרְנֶט הַלֵּל בַּמַּעֲמַקִּים
הַהֲזוּיִּים אַתָּה מוֹפִיעַ כְּרָפָא, בְּצַג הַסֶּלוּלָרִי
הִלַּלְתִּיךְ, בְּהוֹדָעַת הַטֶּקְסְט: תְּקַשֵּׁר דָּחוּף,
וְהִלַּלְתִּיךְ בִּתְשׁוּבַת אָחִי, בַּהֲמִיתוֹ חוֹתֶכֶת הֶעָרִים, רוֹצַעַת אֶת הָאֹזֶן:
אַתָּה חַיָּב לָבוֹא, אֲבִיבָה, אֲבִיבָה מֵתָה.

וְהִלַּלְתִּיךְ, הִלַּלְתִּיךְ,
אוֹרֵז אֶת הַבְּגָדִים, נֶחְבָּט אֶל הַצְּלִילוֹת, רַגְלַי מָטוֹת, הַלֵּל בְּשַׁעֲרֵי
הַפָּתוֹלוֹגְיָה, הַלֵּל אַבּוּ אַבּוּ כַּבִּיר, בִּמְשׁוּכוֹת הָרָדוּף הִלַּלְתִּי,
אֶל מִסְתּוֹרָן אֲנִי וּשְׁנֵי אַחַי חוֹמְקִים לְהִשָּׁבֵר, וּבִתְעוּדַת פְּטִירָה
הִלַּלְתִּי, לֹא מָשׁ מִבֵּין שְׂפָתַי הַלֵּל, נוֹסְעִים מֵאֲחוֹרֵי הָאַמְבּוּלַנְס
הַמּוֹבִילָה הַבַּיְתָה, הִלַּלְתִּי כָּל הַדֶּרֶךְ, חֹרֶף מְפֻזָּר, חֹרֶף נָקִי, חֹרֶף שָׁטוּף
עֶדְנָה, הַלֵּל בְּצֶמֶת נְצָנִים, בְּפִקְק תְּנוּעָה הִלַּלְתִּי, יוֹשְׁבִים
מַאֲזִינִים לְרַחַשׁ הֶפְשָׁרָה, הַקֶּרַח הַנָּמֵס בַּמְכוּלָה בָּהּ גוּפָתָהּ
דְּחוּיַת הַנְּתִיחָה, הַטְּהוֹרָה מֵרַעַל, אוֹסֶפֶת שׁוּב
אֶת רַכּוּתָהּ.

שָׂרַפְךָ
צַו וְיִשְׁאֲלוּ
מִי הַלַּלְךָ עוֹד כֹּה מֵעַל

29

over the tar's timbre, through the asphalt's roar, in an air of slackened honey,

and who had exalted your name with a sister, with her fleeting breath in the bathroom, with a

conquered heart and with flesh lying on the floor, turning blue,

bursting with a splendor of eternal silence, with a mother desperately kissing it

Who had once lauded thee.

זִמְרַת הַזֶּפֶת, מֵעֵבֶר דְּכִי אַסְפַלְט, בִּדְבַשׁ רָפוּי שֶׁל הָאֲוִיר,
וּמִי קַדֵּשׁ שִׁמְךָ בַּאֲחוֹתוֹ, בִּנְשִׁימָתָהּ הַחֲטוּפָה בְּבֵית שִׁמּוּשׁ, בְּלֵב
כָּבוּשׁ וּבְבָשָׂר שׁוֹכֵב עַל הָרִצְפָּה, מַכְחִיל,
נִמְלָא הַדְרַת דּוּמָה, בָּאֵם הַמְכַסָּה אוֹתוֹ בִּנְשִׁיקוֹת
מִי קָלַסְךָ.

9.

At the dawn of *Kislev*

she suddenly knew

the will of the body is the source of the Fall,

not like then, in that ancient story

of knowledge, of flesh, or maybe it's always been

thus—a plea to exceed, to shatter the limit,

only thus will it be met, reaching an other.

How will it reach, if in order to pass it is forced

to cancel its stay. It is slaughtered towards the desire for space,

towards its error of middle-grounds, which thus turn concrete,

which require a linkage that, through affinity, can call out with strength:

get to know us, oh body, and we will be for you.

But she, she knew well, the thing that appears

at the end of the night like a light is

her gate, when darkness is rolled up away

from the world—what does it mean to follow the will of the body;

she had the choice to leave,

to shed off the cold-snaps of the year,

leaving the garden withered and sere,

almond calyxes trapped in follicles, a purple blossom

within the corolla, to undo in her room explosives of chance,

the crestfallen ending of an O. Henry tale,

ט.

בְּשַׁחַר כְּסִלוֹ לְפֶתַע יָדְעָה
רְצוֹן הַגּוּף הוּא יוֹצֵר הַגֵּרוּשׁ,
לֹא כְּמוֹ אָז, בַּסִּפּוּר הַיָּשָׁן
עַל יֶדַע, בָּשָׂר, וְאוּלַי מִתָּמִיד זֶה
הָיָה – תִּחְנֶה לַחֲרֹג, לְשַׁבֵּר אֶת הַגְּבוּל,
שֶׁרַק כָּךְ הוּא יְשֻׁלַּם, כְּשֶׁיֵּצֵא אֶל אַחֵר.
אֵיךְ יֵצֵא, אִם כְּדֵי לַעֲבֹר הוּא מָדַח
אֶל בִּטּוּל הַשְּׁהוּת. הוּא נִטְבָּח אֶל תְּשׁוּקַת הַמֶּרְוָח,
אֶל טָעוּת שְׁרִיתוֹ בַּבֵּינַיִם, הַהוֹפְכִים לְמַמָּשׁ, הַזְּקוּקִים לַזִּקָּה,
רַק הַיַּחַס נוֹתֵן לָהֶם כֹּחַ לִקְרֹא:
הַכִּירֵנוּ, הוֹ, גּוּף, וְנִהְיֶה בִּשְׁבִילְךָ.
אֲבָל הִיא, הִיא יָדְעָה, הַדָּבָר הֶעָשׂוּי
בְּתֻמּוֹ שֶׁל לַיְלָה כְּמוֹ אוֹר הוּא
הַשַּׁעַר שֶׁלָּהּ, בִּגְלִילַת הַחֹשֶׁךְ מִפְּנֵי
הָעוֹלָם – מָה פֵּשֶׁר מִלּוּי רְצוֹנוֹ שֶׁל הַגּוּף:
רְשׁוּתָהּ זוֹ הָיְתָה לַעֲזֹב,
לְהַשִּׁיל מֵעַצְמָהּ אֶת קְרוֹת הַשָּׁנָה
הָעוֹמְדוֹת לוֹחֲצוֹת אֶת צְמִיחַת הַגַּנָּה,
גְּבִיעֵי שָׁקֵד בְּתוֹךְ זְקִיקֵיהֶם, תִּפְרַחַת סְגֻלָּה
בְּתוֹךְ כּוֹתָרוֹת, לִפְרֹק בְּחַדְרָהּ חֲזִיזִים שֶׁל אַקְרַאי
סוֹפוֹ הֶעָגוּם שֶׁל סִפּוּר שֶׁל אוֹ הֶנְרִי,
קַנָּאוּת שֶׁל ז'וּל וֶרְן לִפְרָטֵי הַמַּפּוֹת, צִטּוּט

Jules Verne's acuteness to a fine map's detail, a quote

by Miss Lamb or her husband,

Shakespeare flayed of poetry.

Yes, her permission it was, and thus it shall stay,

because we were plunged into no lesser a chore: to measure

her distance with a heart full of grime, to write down

her movement stripped bare of time—

שֶׁל הַגְּבֶרֶת לֶמְב אוֹ שֶׁל בַּעֲלָהּ,
שֶׁקְסְפִּיר פָּשׁוּט מֵעוּר הַשִּׁירָה.
כֵּן, רְשׁוּתָהּ זוֹ הָיְתָה, וּרְשׁוּתָהּ זוֹ תִּהְיֶה,
כִּי אָנוּ הוּטַלְנוּ לִשְׁהוּת לֹא פְחוּתָהּ: חָשׁוּב
מֵרַחֲקֶיהָ בְּלֵב מִלְבָּן, רָשׁוּם
תְּנוּעָתָהּ הַנְּקִיַּת מִן הַזְּמַן –

10.

The residents discovered the bougainvillea: slender necks, quivering

lips. Calyces

hammered hammered

with tough brightness. The colors

lost their names in showers of sunlight,

in *Tevethian* shards of frost.

Yitgadales and *Yitkadashes*

stole across the garden's end.

ז.

התוֹשָׁבִים גִּלּוּ אֶת הַבּוּגֶנְוִילְיָה: צַוָּארִים דַּקִּים, שְׂפָתַיִם
רוֹטְטוֹת. גְּבִיעִים
רְקוּעִים רְקוּעִים
נִהֲרָה קְשׁוּחָה. הַצְּבָעִים
אִבְּדוּ אֶת שְׁמָם בְּקִלּוּחֵי שֶׁמֶשׁ
בְּמַכְּתוֹת כְּפוֹר מְטַבְּתוֹת.
צְלוֹת וּבָעוּת
גָּנְבוּ אֶת גְּבוּל הַגִּנָּה.

11.

Salvation and fear turned into thorns—

a bird shrieked in the olive tree thicket;

a bird chiseled sound in the rain.

My body succumbed to the inheritance, pulsing: possibilities

of pain, the spilt quiddity

of the blood, whole—

heartedness demanded by others.

יא.

יְשׁוּעָה וּפַחַד הָיוּ לִצְנִינִים –
צִפּוֹר צָלְלָה בִּסְבַךְ עֵץ הַזַּיִת;
צִפּוֹר חָרְצָה קוֹל בַּגֶּשֶׁם.
גּוּפִי נַעֲנָה לַיִּרְשָׁה בְּהֶלֶם: אֶפְשָׁרֻיּוֹת
שֶׁל כְּאֵב, עַצְמוּתוֹ הַשְּׁפוּכָה
שֶׁל הַדָּם, חֵפֶץ –
לֵב שֶׁטָּבְעוּ אֲחֵרִים.

12.

Shevat crept in coils of ice, cracks

of expanding control, a constant zeppelin flickered,

let drop from a god's mind. To give in to it—to capture the predictable

in crystal spheres carrying stars, to register

the bearings' mechanical moans as the nights shift,

a translucent halo rising like vapor from beyond the growth

and its ebbing strength, veil

over veil, sheets of light exposed by their unease, a divination

in larks and strips of clouds—

there is a structure, a design, or at least a demand for

man to bow his head, to slice paths

in the air, to rise above his life

to some height, be as a poet, believing

he will catch in paintings

something of human sorrow. No, not

what you've wanted,

metaphysics is the origin of havoc. To betray

this then—roam the world

as angels deaf to Aramaic,

striving for existence in the body,

to learn how to subside in a *Shevat*

furrowed with frost. The wild carrot is all conceit, its sole purpose

יב.

טִפֵּס שֶׁבֶט בְּקִנּוֹקָנוֹת שֶׁל קֶרַח, סְדָקִים

שֶׁל הַרְחָבַת שִׁלְטוֹן, צֶפֶּלִין־תָּמִיד הַזָּהָב,

שָׁמוּט מִזְּכְרוֹנוּ שֶׁל אֵל. לְהִתְמַסֵּר לָזֶה – לִתְפֹּס אֶת הַצָּפוּי

בְּגַלְגַּלֵּי הַבְּדֹלַח נוֹשְׂאֵי הַכּוֹכָבִים, לִרְשֹׁם

אֶת יְבָבַת הַמַּסַּבִּים כְּשֶׁהַלֵּילוֹת נָעִים,

הִלָּה שְׁקוּפָה עוֹלָה כְּאֵד מֵעֵבֶר לַצְּמִיחָה

וְכוֹחוֹתֶיהָ הַכַּלִּים, צָעִיף

וְעוֹד צָעִיף, אֶת יְרִיעוֹת הָאוֹר תַּסְגִּיר עַצְבָּנוּתָן, נָחוּשׁ

בְּעֶפְרוֹנִים וּרְצוּעוֹת עָנָן

– מַתְכֹּנֶת יֵשׁ, אַדְרִיכָלוּת, אוֹ לְפָחוֹת תְּבִיעָה מִן

הָאָדָם לָשַׂח אֶת רֹאשׁוֹ, לִבְצֹעַ בָּאֲוִיר

שְׁבִילִים, לְהִתְרוֹמֵם מֵעַם חַיָּיו

אֶל אֵיזֶה גֹּבַהּ, לִהְיוֹת כַּמְּשׁוֹרֵר, סָבוּר

שֶׁיִּתְבּוֹנֵן בְּצִיּוּרִים

אֶל תּוֹךְ דָּבָר שֶׁל יִסּוּרֵי אֱנוֹשׁ. לֹא, לֹא

מָה שֶׁרְצִית,

הַמֶּטָפִיזִיקָה תְּהֵא רֵאשִׁית הַחִדָּלוֹן. לַבֶּגֶד

בָּזֶה אִם כֵּן – כְּמַלְאָכִים אֲשֶׁר חֵרְשִׁים

לָאֲרָמִית לָלֶכֶת בָּעוֹלָם,

חוֹתְרִים אֶל מַמָּשׁוּת בַּגּוּף,

לִלְמֹד לְהִצְטַמְצֵם בְּשֵׁבֶט חָרוּשׁ

הַכְּפוֹר. גֶּזֶר הַגַּנָּה הוּא רַק גְּאוֹן שֶׁתַּכְלִיתוֹ

is to bend under the burden of the self, the rose— whirlpool of color, a rustle

fit for fragrancy.

No, not that? What was the flower you desired? The *sheizava*?

Here it is, as you have wished, clear as alcohol,

the effort of its foliage brought a bloody sun above it. And it is ripe—

reach out your hand.

כְּרִיעָה תַּחַת עֲלוֹ שֶׁל הָעַצְמִי, הַוֶּרֶד – מְעַרְבֶּלֶת צֶבַע, אווּש
יָפֶה לַבְּשָׂמִים.
לֹא, לֹא זֶה? מָה הַפֶּרַח שֶׁבְּקַשְׁתְּ? הַשֶּׁיזָבָא?
הִנֵּה הִיא כְּרְעוּתֵךְ צְלוּלָה כְּאַלְכּוֹהוֹל,
בְּטֶרַח עַלְוָתָה זָרְחָה עָלֶיהָ שֶׁמֶשׁ דָּם. וְזוֹהִי עוֹנָתָה -
הוֹשִׁיטִי אֶת יָדֵךְ.

13.

The sun—an old man falls asleep in the sun; the light,

soured milk,

entifies objects. All animals

can endure the endless. But

finitude. In my sleep I do not cease

to hear: lowing, a short sharp

howl, the windy

flicker of the rose's

flame, that quivering

quiver.

יג.

הַשֶּׁמֶשׁ – זָקֵן נִרְדָּם בַּשֶּׁמֶשׁ; חָלָב
שֶׁהֶחְמִיץ הָאוֹר
מְיַשֵּׁשׁ עֲצָמִים. כָּל חַיָּה
בְּכוֹחָהּ לָשֵׂאת אֵינְסוֹף. אֲבָל
הַסּוֹף. בִּשְׁנָתִי לֹא אֶחְדַּל
לִשְׁמֹעַ: גְּעִיָּה, יְלָלָה
דַּקַּת דֶּקֶר, הָזַע
הָרוּחַ אֶת לַהַט
הַוֶּרֶד, הָרַעַד הַהוּא
הָרוֹעֵד.

14.

Where are you? Under a pillow I laid a book

you gave me

my first book

your inscription inside—handwriting clear as

a cut.

My dreams were an empty temple. I waited and waited till

morning.

יד.

הֵיכָן אַתְּ? תַּחַת כַּר הִנַּחְתִּי סֵפֶר
שֶׁנָּתַתְּ לִי
הַסֵּפֶר הָרִאשׁוֹן שֶׁלִּי
הַקְדָּשָׁתֵךְ בַּפֶּתַח – כְּתַב־יָד נָקִי כְּמוֹ
חִתֵּךְ.
הָיוּ חֲלוֹמוֹתַי הֵיכָל רֵיק. חִכִּיתִי וְחִכִּיתִי עַד
הַבֹּקֶר.

Clangs on the anvil of light

that will eventually bisect me

since my birth I hear with woe

Word by word my body is sung

dares dangerously to enter

with my own eyes to know.

(Poetry, 2)

הֲלֹמוּת חִשּׁוּל הָאוֹר
שֶׁיְּבַתְּרֵנִי לְבַסּוֹף
מִלְּדָתִי אֲנִי שׁוֹמֵעַ

מִלָּה מִלָּה גּוּפִי מוּשָׁר
הוֹרֵס אֵלָיו לָבוֹא
בְּמוֹ עֵינַי לְהִתְוַדֵּעַ.

(שִׁירָה, 2)

15.

Let me have those shapes that shrivel language

And I shall break them up limb by limb,

I shall lay bare their roots,

their evil-doings I shall dash against the stone,

malicious sluts say Aviva is gone.

But I was

as well, Hebrew pounding on

my throat-bell, I answered aye.

It has the dick of a camel, that one.

הָבוּ לִי אֶת הַצּוּרוֹת הַמְּצֻרוֹת אֶת הַשָּׂפָה

וַאֲפָרְקֵן אֵיבָר־אֵיבָר,

אֶגְרֹן עַד הַיְסוֹד, מַעֲלָלָן

אֶשְׁבֹּר אֶל סֶלַע,

שֶׁרְמוּטוֹת אֲיֻמּוֹת אוֹמְרוֹת אֲבִיכָה מֵתָה.

אֲבָל הָיִיתִי גַם

אֲנִי, דָּפְקָה עִבְרִית בְּתוֹךְ

גְּרוֹנִי, עָנִיתִי הֵן.

זֹאת זַיִן שֶׁל גָּמָל יֵשׁ לָהּ.

16.

What is wrong with them, the mustard plants, that they are irritated thus all of a sudden,

bellflowers nearing pungency under the oppression of midday

the marigold, it too is burning molecules of oxygen, arising

in their presence like the chariot's celestial wheels.

What season is it now, I do not wish to say: clusters of computers

have yet to flicker information like neurons in a network, skies have

yet to be produced in sweatshops, viewers dumbfounded before them,

letting drop from their mind the children going blind in the process of their welding,

hammers frozen in midair. Is that their noise, coming from outside?

Perhaps it's winter, seems like winter, thunders then, surely

not a sigh

of someone knocking on a door, with no reply,

and the mother then awakens, the door withdrawing in answer to her touch,

she sees – the daughter sitting

dressed in rags of dawn, ready for the journey,

she calls her name, then screams, spraying her with perfume,

the daughter opens up an eye, then lets go. It's done, her voice breaks down, she's gone.

We're now alone, dispatched instead of

I-loved-you-so, a-brother's-duty,

breathing purified air

and the fallow land around flows unblemished—

What is wrong with them, the warblers, that they whisper thus,

מָה יֵשׁ לָהֶם לַחַרְדָּלִים שֶׁכָּךְ הֵם נִרְגָּזִים פִּתְאוֹם,

עֲנָבִים עַזִּים כִּמְעַט בְּלַחַץ צָהֳרַיִם

צִפֹּרֶן הֶחָתוּל גַּם לָהּ שְׂרֵפַת מוֹלְקוּלוֹת חַמְצָן, עוֹלָה

לְעֻמָּתָם כְּאָדָם.

מָה הָעוֹנָה, אֵינִי חָפֵץ לוֹמַר: עוֹד לֹא הִצְבִּיעוּ צְבִירֵי

מַחְשֵׁב מְהַבְהֲבִים מֵידָע כִּרְשָׁתוֹת נוֹיְרוֹנִים, עוֹד לֹא הוּצְאוּ שְׁחָקִים

מִסַּדְנָאוֹת הַיֶּזַע, וְנֶעֶמְדוּ הַמִּשְׁתָּאִים מוּלָם,

שׁוֹמְטִים מִזִּכְרוֹנָם אֶת הַיְּלָדִים הַמְאַבְּדִים רְאוּת בְּחֶשְׁוָלָם,

וּמַקָּבוֹת קְפוּאוֹת בְּהֶגֶף. זֶה רַעַשׁ, הָרְעָשִׁים מִתּוֹךְ הַחוּץ?

אוּלַי בְּעֶצֶם חֹרֶף, נִדְמֶה שֶׁחֹרֶף, וּרְעָמִים אֵפוֹא, וַדַּאי

לֹא נְקִישָׁה

שֶׁל אִישׁ נוֹקֵשׁ עַל דֶּלֶת, לֹא נַעֲנָה,

וּמִקֵּצֶה הָאֵם, לְמַגָּעָהּ הַדֶּלֶת נְסוֹגָה, רוֹאָה – הַבַּת יוֹשֶׁבֶת

לְבוּשָׁה בִּבְלוֹא שֶׁל שַׁחַר, דְּרוּכָה אֶל הַמַּסָּע,

קוֹרֵאת בִּשְׁמָהּ, אַחַר כָּךְ הִיא צוֹעֶקֶת, בְּשֵׁם הִיא מַזֶּה,

הַבַּת פּוֹקַחַת עַיִן, סוֹגַרְתָּהּ. זֶהוּ זֶה, נִשְׁבָּר קוֹלָהּ, הָלְכָה.

אֲנַחְנוּ נִשְׁאַר, מְשֻׁלָּחִים בִּמְקוֹם

אָהַבְתִּי־כָּל־כָּךְ, כְּפִי־חוֹבַתִּי־כָּאָח,

נוֹשְׁמִים אֲוִיר צָרוּף

וּמֶרְחֲבֵי הַבּוֹר סָבִיב זוֹרְמִים בְּטֹהַר - - -

מָה יֵשׁ לָהֶם לַפַּשּׁוֹשִׁים שֶׁכָּךְ הֵם רוֹחֲשִׁים,

מֵחֻכָּם גִּצִּים נוֹרִים, זֶה זָהָרָם, הַזֹּהַר הַמֵּמֵס אֶת הַגְּבוּלוֹת?

from their friction sparks flare out, is that their radiance that melts down all the borders?

Spring fades into summer, gold eddies

on the leaves, not that gold of rings slipped off

from a daughter's dead fingers, not that necklace

bursting bright in the shop windows of London, somewhere close

to Baker street. A bright cargo,

time-of-then bridled in gold:

I am not sixteen enough, the moment of goodbye

was not yet desecrated, you will not yet give words of advice,

not yet command, remember:

to write you must trace

the halting place of your heart,

nearing there backwards

is poetry's art.

אָבִיב נָמוֹג אֶל קַיִץ, זָהָב הַמְפַכְפֵּךְ
עַל הֶעָלִים, לֹא זְהַב הַטַּבָּעוֹת הַמְשֻׁלּוֹת
מֵאֶצְבָּעוֹת מֵתוֹת שֶׁל בַּת, לֹא הָרָבִיד
הַמִּתְפָּרֵץ בָּרָק בְּחַלּוֹנוֹת הָרַאֲוָה שֶׁל לוֹנְדוֹן, הֵיכַנְשֶׁהוּ סָמוּךְ
לִבֵּיקֶר סְטְרִיט. זָהָב,
מֻטְעָן בָּהִיר, זְמַן־אָז אָסוּר בְּפָז:
אֵינִי מַסְפִּיק בֶּן שֵׁשׁ־עֶשְׂרֵה, הָרֶגַע לַפְּרֵדָה
עוֹד לֹא חָלַל, עוֹד לֹא תִּתְּנִי עֵצָה לַדֶּרֶךְ,
וְלֹא תּוֹרִי זָכוֹר,
כְּדֵי לִכְתֹּב אַתָּר
הֵיכָן לִבֵּךְ עוֹמֵד,
הַהִתְקָרְבוּת הַלֹּא נִגְמֶרֶת חֲזָרָה
זוֹ הַשִּׁירָה.

17.

And I once already learned
to live off poetry.
I labored to discern
the chrysanthemums' haste
from seared angels
crucified on stems,
swallows boasting on air
from crumbs of coal.
I knew which would be harder,
the Fall
down from bliss
up from Terra—

יז.

וּפַעַם כְּבָר לָמַדְתִּי
לִחְיוֹת מִן הַשִּׁירָה.
שֶׁכְלַלְתִּי לְהַבְדִּיל
פַּחַז חַרְצִיּוֹת מִמַּלְאָכִים צְרוּבִים
צְלוּבִים עַל גִּבְעוֹלִים,
סִיסֵי חוֹמוֹת מִתְפָּאֲרִים עַל הָאֲוִיר
מֵחֲתִיכוֹת פֶּחָם.
יָדַעְתִּי מָה קָשָׁה יוֹתֵר
הַנְּפִילָה
מַטָּה מֵעֵדְנָה
מַעְלָה מֵאַרְעָא –

18.

But if compelled to give form to

my sister— and if I ask someone

to name a force of nature,

surely then a word

will be replaced with

a reply, a desire

to be a construct, a contradiction,

and I'll be answered, always answered thus:

a pillar of storm or the heavy heat of *Tammuz* or

the lily's sepal breaking through a bed of *Kurkar* sand—

how will I, then, how will I speak

her.

יח.

אַךְ אִם אֲנִי אָנוּס לָתֵת דְּמוּת
לַאֲחוֹתִי – וְאִם אֶשְׁאַל אֵי מִי
לוֹמַר לִי כֹּחַ טֶבַע מָה
הֲלוֹא אָז תִּתְחַלֵּף מִלָּה
בְּפִתְרוֹן, תְּשׁוּקָה
לִהְיוֹת בִּנְיָן, סְתִירָה,
וְאֶעֱנֶה, תָּמִיד כָּךְ נַעֲנֶה:
עַמּוּד סוּפָה אוֹ שָׁרָב תַּמּוּז אוֹ
גְּבִיעַ חֲבַצֶּלֶת שׁוֹבֵר מַצַּע כָּרְכָּר –
כֵּיצַד אֲנִי, אִם כֵּן, אֵיךְ אֲדַבֵּר
אוֹתָהּ.

19.

One can sing of rain, the mightiness
of water, all through the shiv'ah corpulent clouds
rubbed against the softness
of the mourners' tent, and of the slightest of them one can sing,
now on the dawn of *Shevat*,
infidel frost over the greyish lawn, there your childhood,
and there your fallen life is crammed:

Your locks are full of shards
after a shower, through which you've run your fingers
and did not brush, even when they chided, a smile on your lips,
you read Austen, that British bitch has
a sharp wit, as fog dwellers usually do, outline of geography,

and a teacher's comments of amazement, reddish
upon the copied desert maps, distances
you've crossed, fixed within Sderot, asphalt lines
reaching your students, disquieting problems
of geometry.

Could you have guessed all this was
before you came to know it,

אֶפְשָׁר לָשִׁיר עַל גְּשָׁמִים, גְּבוּרוֹת
הַמַּיִם, כָּל הַשִּׁבְעָה כִּרְסֵי הָעֲנָנִים
חָכְכוּ בְּרֹךְ חֵפַת
הָאֲבֵלִים, וְעַל הַדַּק מֵהֶם אֶפְשָׁר לָשִׁיר,
עַכְשָׁו בִּשְׁחַר שְׁבָט,
כְּפַר עַל דֶּשֶׁא אֲפַרְפַּר, שָׁם יַלְדוּתֵךְ,
וְשָׁם חַיַּיִךְ הַמֵּתִים דְּחוּקִים:

קוּצוֹתַיִךְ מְלֵאוֹת שְׁבָרִים
מִן הַמִּקְלַחַת, שֶׁהֶעֱבַרְתְּ בָּן אֶת יָדֵךְ
וְלֹא סָרַקְתְּ, גַּם כְּשֶׁהֵעִירוּ, חִיּוּךְ עַל שְׂפָתוֹתַיִךְ,
קָרֵאת בְּאוֹסְטֶן, חוּשׁ הוּמוֹר מְשֻׁחָז יֵשׁ
לַכַּלְבָּה הַבְּרִיטִית, בִּכְלָל לָהֶם יוֹשְׁבֵי הָעֲרָפֶל, סְכוּם בְּגֵאוֹגְרַפְיָה,

וְסִמּוּנֵי הַהִשְׁתָּאוּת שֶׁל הַמּוֹרָה, אֲדֻמּמַּיִם עַל
הַמַּפּוֹת הַמְּעֻתָּקוֹת שֶׁל הַמִּדְבָּר, מְרַחֲקִים
שֶׁאַתְּ צָלַחְתְּ, קְבוּעִים בְּתוֹךְ שְׂדֵרוֹת, קַוֵּי אַסְפַלְט
מִמֵּךְ אֶל תַּלְמִידַיִךְ, סְגִיּוֹת עוֹכְרוֹת שַׁלְוָה
בְּגֵאוֹמֶטְרִיָה.

הַאִם שִׁעַרְתְּ שֶׁכָּל זֶה כְּבָר הָיָה
בְּטֶרֶם הִתְוַדַּעְתְּ לוֹ,

because the future has occurred and it's blowing

your way you

who are time resistant—

The end of time has wakened, will

you not hear, in the air's fortress,

among the dewdrops, the almond tree quivers at its blossoms, no,

it has quivered,

no, the planted trees have dried out, the growing flora have expired, the earth has vomited

its heart, and it's enormous,

breathing your breath, light had descended like iron,

so refined, filled its space below

the whole world has broken so, facing Aviva-no.

כִּי הֶעָתִיד אֱרַע וְהוּא נוֹשֵׁב
אֵלַיִךְ אֶת
הָעֲמִידָה לַזְּמַן –

קֵץ הַיָּמִים הֵקִיץ, הַאִם
לֹא תִשְׁמְעִי, בְּתוֹךְ מִבְצַר הָאֲוִירִים,
בֵּין הַטְּלָלִים, הַשְּׁקֵדִיָּה נִרְעֶדֶת מִפְּרִיחָה, לֹא,
הִיא נִרְעָדָה,

לֹא, הָעֵצִים הַנִּטָּעִים יָבְשׁוּ, כַּלְתָה הַצִּמְחִיָּה אֲשֶׁר תִּצְמַח, הָאֲדָמָה הֵקִיאָה
אֶת לִבָּהּ, וְהוּא עֲנָק
נוֹשֵׁם אֶת נִשְׁמָתֵךְ, הָאוֹר יָרַד כְּבַרְזִלִּים,
הָדוּר כָּל כָּךְ, מָלֵא אֶת חֲלָלוֹ
הָעוֹלָם הִכְרַע כֻּלּוֹ אֶל מוּל אֲבִיבָה-לֹא.

20. _____

A stretched glimmer is the glass
on the window, bliss it was
deserted in that grove.

I took a stone—
a piece
she scorched for me
said I should look
through it at the sun.

It was a eucalyptus grove,
its scent awakened, waned.
Its flames idle, rustling,
green glint burst
from them, drowned

in a light hard with soot,
a little cloud. Thirty
years my back was turned to
her moment of escape

כ.

נִיצוֹץ מָתוּחַ הַזְּכוּכִית
עַל פְּנֵי הַחַלּוֹן, חֶמְדָּה הָיְתָה
בְּחֹרֶשׁ עֲזוּבָה.

אֲנִי לָקַחְתִּי אֶבֶן, הִיא –
פִּסָּה
חָרְכָה לְמַעֲנִי
אָמְרָה לִי לְהַבִּיט
בַּשֶּׁמֶשׁ בַּעֲדָהּ.

הָיָה חֹרֶשׁ אֵיקָלִיפְּטוּס,
רֵיחוֹ הַקַּיִץ, כָּבָה.
לְהָבָיו נִרְפִּים, מְאֻוְשִׁים,
בְּרַק יָרֹק זֶנֶק גָּמִישׁ
מֵהֶם, טֶבַע

בְּאוֹר נְחוּשׁ כְּפִיחַ,
עֲנָנָה, שְׁלוֹשִׁים
שָׁנָה גַּבֵּי הוּסַב אֶל
זְמַן חֲמִיקָתָהּ

towards what, towards some truth:

In these reins—

love—

lies the utter power to release us from ourselves

but so they also mean

to place in another's hands

the right to make us lonely.

לְעֵבֶר מָה, לְאֵיזוֹ יְדִיעָה:

בַּמּוֹסֵרוֹת הָאֵלֶּה –
אַהֲבָה –
הַכּוֹחַ הַגָּמוּר לְהַתִּירֵנוּ מֵעַצְמֵנוּ
מִשּׁוּם כָּךְ גַּם פֵּרוּשָׁן
לָתֵת בִּידֵי אַחֵר רְשׁוּת
לַעֲשׂוֹתֵנוּ בּוֹדְדִים.

21.

The body knew what it knew
and kept silent.

Trees spoke. The sun spoke
with heightened
courage. Night divided
into shifts of poetry.

The wind swept away the murmur,
God's stars eroded like
bones.

And she smiled, withdrew from the moon held
between the thumb and the forefinger, its light
diluted in the television's glow. She smiled,
Men achieved all that, American footsteps in space,
prints of dust and time.

She smiled, knitting patterns into
yarmulkes with one needle. She smiled when sketching
them on graphing paper, in those cages of squares,
smiled when her girls came

כא.

הַגּוּף יָדַע מָה שֶׁיָּדַע
וְהֶחֱרִישׁ.

עֵצִים דִּבְּרוּ. דִּבֵּר הַשֶּׁמֶשׁ
בִּגְבוּרָה
גְּבוֹהָה. לַיְלָה נֶחְלַק
לְמִשְׁמְרוֹת שִׁירָה.

הָרוּחַ טִאְטְאָה אֶת הַמִּלְמוּל,
כּוֹכְבֵי יָהּ שְׂחוּקִים כְּמוֹ
עֲצָמוֹת.

וְהִיא חִיכָה, מִן הַיָּרֵחַ נְסוֹגָה, אָחוּז
בֵּין אֲגוּדָל וְאֶצְבַּע, אוֹרוֹ
נִמְהָל בְּאוֹר הַטֶּלֶוִיזְיָה. חִיכָה,
יַד אָדָם הִשִּׂיגָה אֶת כָּל זֶה, סְלִיוֹת חָלָל אֲמֶרִיקָאִיּוֹת,
טְבִיעוֹת אָבָק וּזְמַן.

חִיכָה, סוֹרֶגֶת דְּגָמָאוֹת לְתוֹךְ
כַּפּוֹת בְּמַסְרֵגָה אַחַת. חִיכָה גַם כְּשֶׁתִּכְּנָה
אוֹתָן בְּמַחְבְּרוֹת חֶשְׁבּוֹן, בִּכְלוּב הַמִּשְׁבְּצוֹת,
חִיכָה כְּשֶׁבָּאוּ תַּלְמִידוֹת מִן הַכִּתָּה

tortured in starched blouses, in their burning virginity, copying

notes: forms and languages. She smiled, for years she has

been leaving

things to their images.

Attila lashed into the wilderness like a whip, like dawn, like

birds, the Greeks and their logic, their palpable

passion, Assyria cut through with razors of fire,

these were all fluctuations on an axis,

a flowchart.

Then she went

to Tel Aviv by bus. An enthused young man

apprised her of the

information age—pinheads,

digits compressed in nonspace,

the speed of light.

She returned. It was waiting, that same house, where her mother

brought her forth. It expected her, the room,

ready to receive her own *tzimtzum*. And she

smiled, it was

סְגוּפוֹת בְּסַד חֶלְצָה, בִּבְתוּלֵיהֶן הַבּוֹעֲרִים, הֶעְתִּיקוּ
סְכוּמִים: מִבְּנִים וּלְשׁוֹנוֹת. חִיכָה, שָׁנִים שֶׁהִיא
הִנִּיחָה
אֶת הַדְּבָרִים לִדְמוּיָם.

אֲטִילָה הַמֻּצְלָף בָּעֲרָבוֹת כְּמוֹ שׁוֹט, כְּמוֹ שַׁחַר, כְּמוֹ
צִפּוֹר, הַיָּנִים וְהִגְיוֹנָם, תְּשׁוּקָתָם הַמוּחָשִׁית
כָּל כָּךְ, אַשּׁוּר הַחֲתוּכָה בְּתַעַר אֵשׁ,
כֻּלָּם הָיוּ תְּנוּדָה עַל צִיר,
תַּרְשִׁים זְרִימָה.

אַחַר כָּךְ גַּם נָסְעָה
בָּאוֹטוֹבּוּס לְתֵל אָבִיב. בָּחוּר נִרְגָּשׁ
בִּשֵּׂר לָהּ עַל רֵאשִׁית
עֵדֶן הָאִינְפוֹרְמַצְיָה — רָאשֵׁי סְכָּה,
סְפָרוֹת דְּחוּסוֹת בְּאֵינְהַחֲלָל,
מְהִירוּת אוֹר.

חֲזָרָה. הַמְתִּין אוֹתוֹ הַבַּיִת, שָׁם חִבְּלָתָה
אִמָּהּ. חִכָּה הַחֶדֶר
נָכוֹן לִקְלֹט אֶת צִמְצוּמָהּ. וְהִיא
חִיכָה, הָיָה

raining outside the window, thundered air, the mistake has just been known

Men

were sure

that history

had a purpose of its own.

גָּשׁוּם מֵעֵבֶר לַחַלּוֹן, אֲוִיר רָעוּם, הַטָּעוּת זֶה הַשְׁלְמָה

בְּנֵי אָדָם

הָיוּ בְּטוּחִים

שֶׁלַהִיסְטוֹרְיָה

יֵשׁ תַּכְלִית בִּפְנֵי

עַצְמָהּ.

22.

I recall the flame tree made taut with summer
in Sderot,
its reddish dawn is also
a Strip of fire.

Nothing's scorched, skin
nor sight: it's here we came, my sweaty
palm clawed
in yours.

And here you set me down, showed me
the books. A braid you had,
there were your eyes, you did not know
how redeemed
you were already.

Thirteen years old, delivered from
the flesh, breathing air whose
nature is unknown. And the world
trembled, the world raged, thrusts of light
like chariots. You grasped
the movement, the dismemberment, you raised

כב.

זָכַרְתִּי אֶת עֵץ הַצַּאֱלוֹן נְדָרֵךְ בַּקַּיִץ
שֶׁל שְׂדֵרוֹת,
אַדְמַת קְטִיפָתוֹ גַּם הִיא
אֵשׁ רְצוּעָה.

דָּבָר אֵינוּ נֶחֱרָךְ, לֹא הָעוֹר,
הָרְאָיָה: לְכָאן בָּאנוּ, כַּף
יָדִי הַמָּזִיעָה צְבוּתָה
בְּכַף יָדֵךְ.

וְכָאן הוֹשַׁבְתְּ אוֹתִי מוּל
הַסְּפָרִים. צַמָּה הָיְתָה לָךְ,
הָיוּ עֵינַיִךְ, וְלֹא יָדַעְתְּ
כַּמָּה אַתְּ כְּבָר
גְּאוּלָה.

בַּת שְׁלוֹשׁ-עֶשְׂרֵה, שְׁלוּחָה
מִן הַבָּשָׂר, נוֹשֶׁמֶת אֲוִיר אֲשֶׁר
טִיבוֹ עָלוּם. וְהָעוֹלָם
נִרְעַד, הָעוֹלָם סָאַן, תְּנוּפוֹת שֶׁל אוֹר
כְּרַכְבִים. תָּפַסְתְּ
אֶת הַתְּנוּעָה, אֶת הַבָּתוֹר, נָשָׂאת

75

your eyes but horizon there was none,

cranes of warblers lashed the ground,

and dandelion scaffolds

cling, reaching where.

Thirty years you lingered in the here. Walked with us

a touch at most, almost

never tempted by the human din. We in the profanum vulgus

racing through urban sprawl, crossing seas –

Paris, Florence, London, a bundle of appalling flesh and marble, which did not

cease with your cessation

and you're with us, at our side, in your here, craving

love, casting sentences over the distance,

but never shackled.

We knew you utterly without knowing

one fraction. If redemption is losing

the self, then who is

the redeemed.

מַבָּט וְאֹפֶק לֹא הָיָה,
עֲגוּרָנִים שֶׁל פָּשׁוֹשִׁים צָלְפוּ בַּתַּחְתִּיּוֹת
וּפְגוּמֵי שֵׁן הָאֲרִי
נֶאֱחָזִים, עוֹלִים לְאָן.

שְׁלוֹשִׁים שָׁנָה נוֹתֶרֶת בְּכָאן. הָלַכְתְּ אִתָּנוּ
רַק מְעַט, כִּמְעַט
וְלֹא נִפְתֵּית לְרַחַשׁ הָאֱנוֹשׁ. אֲנַחְנוּ בַּפְּרוֹפָנוּם וּלְגוּס
שֶׁעָטְנוּ בַּכְּרַכִּים, חָצִינוּ אֶת הַיָּם –
פָּרִיז, פִירֶנְצֶה, לוֹנְדוֹן, גְּבוּבִים שֶׁל גּוּף וְשַׁיִשׁ נִתְעָבִים, שֶׁלֹּא
חָדְלוּ עִם הֶחָדֵלֶךְ

וְאַתְּ אִתָּנוּ, מִן הַצַּד, בְּכָאן שֶׁלָּךְ, שׁוֹעָה
לְאַהֲבָה, מוֹתַחַת מִשְׁפָּטִים עַל הַמֶּרְחָק,
אֲבָל לֹא אֲסוּרָה.

הִכַּרְנוּ אֶת כֻּלֵּךְ בְּלִי לְהַכִּיר שׁוּם
פְּרָט. אִם גְּאֻלָּה הִיא אִבַּדְנוּ
שֶׁל הָעַצְמִי, מִי
זֶה שֶׁנִּגְאַל.

23.

Fine as sea amidst a summered winter
swarms of sun stream into
the stir

Fine as a dim ascent, the stab
of crows across a streetlight,
battered

Fine as a galvanized fence
cutting down the shoreline of
Jaffa

Fine as the word fine
in the flea market, clamoring against
an iron shield

Fine as a polished blade
at home, like the coiled
step walking towards it

כג.

דַּקָּה כְּמוֹ יָם בְּחֹרֶף מְקַיֵּץ
וּנְחִילֵי חַמָּה שׁוֹטְפִים אֶל
הַתְּנוּעָה

דַּקָּה כְּמוֹ נְסִיקָה כֵּהָה, דְּקִירַת
עוֹרֵב מֵעַל פָּנָס רְחוֹב
חָבוּל

דַּקָּה כְּמוֹ מָסַךְ פַּח מְגֻלְוָן
כּוֹרֵת בְּקַו הַחוֹף שֶׁל
יָפוֹ

דַּקָּה כְּמוֹ הַמִּלָּה דַּקָּה
בְּשׁוּק הַפִּשְׁפְּשִׁים, מַרְעֶשֶׁת מוּל
מָגֵן בַּרְזֶל

דַּקָּה כְּמוֹ לַהַב
הַלָּטוּשׁ בַּבַּיִת, כְּמוֹ צַעַד
הַקָּפוּץ בַּהֲלִיכָה אֵלָיו

Finest of

the fine, fine as a threshold,

as a cut of fear that I might

join

the legions whose grief

turns to bitterness over their own demise.

דַּקָּה מִן
הַדַּקָּה, דַּקָּה כְּמוֹ מִפְתָּן,
כְּמוֹ חִתּוּךְ אֵימָה שֶׁמָּא

אֶפְסַע
אֶל לִגְיוֹנוֹת שֶׁלֶּכֶת אֲהוּבָם
הָיְתָה לִמְרִדָה עַל אָבְדָנָם שֶׁלָם.

24.

Noooooo, pain, don't let go—my heart, don't cease in sorrow,

blood, boil, flare, murmur

and body, burn, burn, the nerves winding through the flesh, and you too muscles,

catch fire, bones chafing the innards,

pinch, scratch them some, so that abscess will emerge

thus I shall not ask where her memory is—what oblivion might mime,

thus I shall not let slip between my hands

a sister into time.

כד.

לאאאאא, אַל תַּרְפֶּה כְּאֵב, לִבִּי, אַל תַּעֲמֹד מִצַּעַר,
דָּם לָהַט, רָתַח, אוּש
וְגוּף, בְּעַר, בְּעַר, הָעֲצַבִּים הַמִּשְׁתָּרְגִים לְאֹרֶךְ הַבָּשָׂר, וְגַם אַתֶּם שְׁרִירִים,
עֲלוּ בָאֵשׁ, הָעֲצָמוֹת הַמִּתְחַכְּכוֹת בָּאֵיבָרִים הַפְּנִימִיִּים,
דְּקָרוּ, גָּרְדוּ בָּהֶם מְעַט וְתַעֲלֶה מֻרְסָה
וּבַל אֶשְׁאַל הֵיכָן זִכְרָהּ, שֶׁכְחָתָהּ אֵי אָן
בַּל אֶשָּׁמֵט מִבֵּין יָדַי
אָחוֹת אֶל תּוֹךְ הַזְּמַן.

25.

Here you are. Revealed to me molded in the flesh
of Patti Smith, ancient eyes
of poetry, a throat chafed with dust,
time woven from sleep.

Over the pulse
of Tel Aviv and Jaffa, whose electrum
wanes and they have voice: in the bus
I am asked, where is His Glory's place? A hellish country, moaning
in the streets, Cyprus wine, Karshina lye,
why are they used, asks the merchant,
and the neighbor rants unaware in Arabic
Wu'natalti ruha u'shmait batrai kal zia sagi—

Resting in center-sky
a living creature named Aviva, and your forehead
carved with words. A galaxy gliding
through like a fleet of spaceships,
in inverted brightness, like platelets drowning
in a stream of Adolan, they too have melody,
they too sing

כה.

הִנָּךְ. נִגְלֵית לִי מִכֵּרֵת מִבְּשָׂרָהּ
שֶׁל פָּאטִי סְמִית', עֵינַיִם עַתִּיקוֹת
שֶׁל הַשִּׁירָה, גָּרוֹן חֲרוּץ עָפָר,
זְמַן קָלוּעַ מִשְׁנֶה.

מֵעַל לִפְעִימָתָן
שֶׁל תֵּל אָבִיב וְיָפוֹ, שֶׁחַשְׁמַלָּן
נֶחְלַשׁ וְהֵן דּוֹבְרוֹת: בָּאוֹטוֹבּוּס
אֲנִי נִשְׁאָל, אַיֵּה מְקוֹם כְּבוֹדוֹ. וּמְדִינָה שֶׁל גֵּהִנָּם, נֶאֱנָחִים
בָּרְחוֹב, יַיִן קַפְרִיסִין, בְּרִית כְּרֵשִׁינָה,
לָמָה בָּאִים הַשָּׁנִים, נִדְרֶשֶׁת זַבְנִית,
וְהַשָּׁכֵן הַמִּתְפָּרֵץ פִּתְאוֹם בַּעֲרָבִית
וּנְטַלְתַּנִי רוּחָא וּשְׁמָעִית בַּתְרַי קָל זִיעַ שַׂגִּיא –

עוֹמֶדֶת בְּמֶרְכַּז רָקִיעַ
חַיָּה וּשְׁמֵךְ אֲבִיבָה, וְעַל מִצְחֵךְ
כָּתוּב. גָּלַקְסִיָה מַחֲלִיקָה
סָבִיב כְּצִי חֲלָלִיּוֹת
בְּנֹגַהּ מְהֻפָּךְ, כִּטַסִּיּוֹת טוֹבְעוֹת
בְּשֶׁטֶף אָדֹלָן, גַּם לָהֶן שִׁיר,
גַּם הֵן שָׁרוֹת

Birds floundering

between you and the city's brim, till they're scattered

by the hollow voice of your reply,

They leave only a puff behind, a soft stroke

against the windows of my room.

Suddenly I know

what it might mean, to awake

on the shore of dawn,

as light trickles in,

facing the bathroom mirror, pressed for by the body—

you are cold and you are lonely

and there is no angel to cry out in your ear

Arise, Live.

צִפּוֹרִים מְגַשְׁשׁוֹת
בֵּינֵךְ וּבֵין מִתְאָר הָעִיר, וּנְפוֹצוֹת מֵרִיק הַקּוֹל
שֶׁל תְּשׁוּבָתֵךְ אֵלַי,

נוֹתַר מֵהֶן רַק הֶדֶף, רַק חֲבָטָה רַכָּה
כְּנֶגֶד חַלּוֹנוֹת חַדְרִי.
פִּתְאֹם אֲנִי יוֹדֵעַ
מָה פֵּרוּשׁוֹ שֶׁל זֶה, לְהִתְעוֹרֵר
עַל שִׂרְטוּטוֹ שֶׁל שַׁחַר,
בִּדְלִיפָתוֹ שֶׁל אוֹר,
מוּל הָרְאִי בַּשֵּׁרוּתִים, לְהִתָּבַע לַגּוּף –
קַר לָךְ וְאַתְּ בּוֹדֵדָה
וְאֵין מַלְאָךְ שֶׁיִּצְעַק לָךְ בְּאָזְנַיִךְ
קוּמִי וַחֲיִי.

26.

Forty-three years old, you are the woman you will always be.

The forehead still unwrinkled. Your eyes well cradled in their orbits. From

the iris looms a meteoric spark, ramming against the void, slicing

up the space, breaking through a crystalline crust of atmosphere. Amino

acids rush to fuse, hasten to secure their strength. Heavy

mammals step out of the sea, send a famished stare

at the titans of all times. Trees quivering with the thrill, a blazing ball whirling

above them, radiating from its spin the lethal ire, music, a lash

of mercy, ideologies pounding as their wheels of thought go round, a breathless race

whose purpose is just you, in the fatherly heart of broiling Av. Heavy heat shatters in air like

splendor, like bones, like fashion. Three and forty years

the light web's bliss cuts your body,

you look with wonder at your feet,

more memory than flesh.

‫כו.‬

בַּת אַרְבָּעִים וְשָׁלוֹשׁ, אַתְּ הָאִשָּׁה שֶׁתִּהְיִי כָּל שְׁאָר חַיַּיִךְ.
הַמֵּצַח עוֹד חָלָק. עֵינַיִךְ שְׁקוּעוֹת נָכוֹן בָּאֲרֻבּוֹת. מִתּוֹךְ
הַקַּשְׁתִּיּוֹת נִבָּט שְׁבִיב מְטָאוֹר, הַהוּא הַמְּנֻגָּשׁ בּוּקָה, חוֹתֵךְ
אֶת הֶחָלָל, מַבְקִיעַ קְרוּם גָּבִישׁ שֶׁל אַטְמוֹסְפֶּרָה. חֶמְצוֹת
אָמִינוֹ נֶחְפָּזוֹת לְהִתְרַכֵּב, אָצוֹת אֶל הַבְטָחַת כּוֹחָן. יוֹנְקִים
כְּבֵדִים פּוֹסְעִים הַחוּצָה מִן הַיָּם, נוֹתְנִים מַבָּט מֵרְעַב
בַּעֲנָקֵי הַזְּמַן. עֵצִים מְצַמְרָרִים מִן הָרִגְשָׁה, כַּדּוּר בּוֹעֵר סְחַרְחַר
מֵעֲלֵיהֶם וּכְבָר קְרוֹנוֹת מִסִּבּוּבוֹ חֲמַת הָרֶצַח, מוּסִיקָה, צְלִיפָה
שֶׁל חֶסֶד, אִידֵאוֹלוֹגִיוֹת מוֹעֲכוֹת בְּגַלְגַּלֵּי מַחְשַׁבְתָּן, מֵרוֹץ נִמְהָר
שֶׁתַּכְלִיתוֹ הוּא אַתְּ, בְּלֵב אָב מְרֻתָּח. שָׁרָב שׁוֹבֵר אֶת הָאֲוִיר כְּמוֹ נֵס,
כְּמוֹ עֲצָמוֹת, כְּמוֹ אָפְנָה. שָׁלוֹשׁ וְאַרְבָּעִים שָׁנָה
עֶדְנַת רִשְׁתוֹת הָאוֹר חוֹרֶצֶת עַל גּוּפֵךְ,
אַתְּ מִסְתַּכֶּלֶת בְּרַגְלַיִךְ בְּתַמְהָה,
פָּחוֹת בָּשָׂר מִזִּכָּרוֹן.

27.

Her laughter, even a twitch of the lip, the weight
of the earth's foundation
in gold.

What shall encompass them—

Children's sweat, lash of labor, stir
of supply, market fusing in another, columns of
economy, words turning to letters,
electric, pulsing in cyber space

and the world is netted with forces of gravity
of a human kind—

Adar unfolds in melded skies,
a blaze of tungsten
in kitchen knives.

כז.

צְחוֹקָה, אֲפִלּוּ נִיד שְׂפָתַיִם, מְשַׁקֵּל
מוֹסְדוֹת הָאָרֶץ
בְּזָהָב.

מָה יְכִילֵם –

זֵעַת הַיְלָדִים, צְלִיפוֹת יְצוּר, זִיעַ
הַסְּחוֹרָה, שׁוּק מִתְגַּלְגֵּל בְּשׁוּק, וּמְדוֹרֵי
הַכַּלְכָּלָה, מִלִּים הוֹפְכוֹת לְאוֹתִיּוֹת
חַשְׁמַל, דְּפָקִים בְּסִיבֵּר הֶחָלָל

וְהָעוֹלָם רֶשֶׁת כֹּחוֹת כְּבֵידָה
מִמִּין אֱנוֹשׁ –

אֲדָר נִפְקַח, רָקִיעַ מְסֻגְסָג זָרֵחַ:
לַהַט טוּנְגְּסְטֶן חָסוּם
בְּסַכִּינֵי מִטְבָּח.

28.

Just before I fell asleep I think

I soot right in a language where

I am deft to the pulse of words:

Darkly I roam Sderot city, technobabble with crows,

fragments of Shakespeare, old kings

carry der doters, battlefields, ghosts of the blood

I bump into you. You don't seem to know me

but you are polite, you tell me the time, you give me

directions, confused,

you catch light with sound, you laugh

me off to echoes of morning. Here I am standing

behind poetry-glazed

glass as a self

pounding, pounding, pounding, as you go bye.

כח.

גֶ׳סְט בִּיפוֹר אַי פוֹל אַסְלִיפ, אַי טְ׳יֶנְק

אַי שׁוֹד וְרַיִט אִין אַ לַנְגְוִיג׳ וֶר

אַי אָם דֶף טוּ דֶה פּוֹלְס אוֹף וֶורְדְס:

דַרְקְלִי אַי רוֹאָם שְׂדֵרוֹת סִיטִי, טֶכְנוֹבֶּבֶּלְד וִיט׳ קְרוֹאוֹס,

פְרַגְמֶנְטְס אוֹף שֶׁקְסְפִּיר, אוֹלְד קִינְגְס

קֶרִי דֶר דוֹאוֹטֶרְס, בַּטְלְפִילְדְס, גוֹסְטְס אוֹף דֶה בְּלָד.

אַי בַּמְפ אִינְטוּ יוּ. יוּ דוֹנְט סִים טוּ נוֹ מִי

בָּט יוּ אָר פּוֹלַיִט, יוּ טֶל מִי דֶה טַיִם, יוּ גִיב מִי

דַיְרֶקְשֶׁנְס, קוֹנְפִיוּזֶד,

יוּ קֶץ׳ לַיִט וִיט׳ סָאוּנְד, יוּ לָף

מִי אוֹף טוּ אֶקוֹס אוֹף מוֹרְנִינְג הִיר אַי אָם סְטַנְדִינְג

בִּיהַיְנְד פּוֹאָטְרִי־גְלֵיזֶד

גְלַסְד אָז אַ סֶלְף

פָאוּנְדִינְג, פָאוּנְדִינְג, פָאוּנְדִינְג, אָז יוּ גוֹ בַּי.

It was once already
said— no!

ever since the wind was hung
upon the willows

and objects are devoured by their
calm:

the sun extinguished since its wick was spared,
making charcoal and harm.

(unhand, 3)

פַּעַם נֶאֱמַר
כְּבָר – לֹא!

מֵאָז עַל עֲרָבִים
תְּלוּיָה הָרוּחַ

וַחֲפָצִים טוֹרֵף
הַשָּׁאֲרָם:

הַשֶּׁמֶשׁ הַשָּׁחוּט עַל פְּתִילָתוֹ שֶׁחָסוּ
וְהוּא עוֹשֶׂה פֶּחָם.

(עֲזֹב, 3)

29.

We were sentenced to be haunted all our days by the tree of the Jews,

that the skies would be shattered by its form,

that beneath the suns—such an exquisite circuit, such a tide of brightness—

its pungency would storm—

What is the scent of memory if not the scent of mourning.

In our veins a nation dreading swamps, addicted to

the dust, whose yearning is twofold:

peace and vengeance;

now we've learned what it is that binds them

into one.

כט.

נִגְזַר לָנוּ שֶׁהַיָּמִים יִהְיוּ מְרֻדָּפִים בְּעֵץ הַיְּהוּדִים,
שֶׁהַשָּׁמַיִם יִשָּׁבְרוּ בְּצוּרָתוֹ,
שֶׁתַּחַת לַשְּׁמָשׁוֹת – סִבּוּב עָנָג כָּזֶה, גֵּאוּת כָּזוֹ שֶׁל זֹהַר –
תָּבוֹא חֲרִיפוּתוֹ –

מָה נִיחוֹחוֹ שֶׁל זִכָּרוֹן אִם לֹא נִיחוֹחַ אֵבֶל.
בְּעוֹרְקֵינוּ עַם יָרֵא בְּצֹאת, מָכוּר אֶל
הֶעָפָר, שֶׁתְּשׁוּקָתוֹ הִיא שְׁתַּיִם:

שָׁלוֹם וּנְקָמָה;
עַתָּה לָמַדְנוּ אֵי זֶה הַדָּבָר הַמַּכְפִּיפָן
בְּיַחַד.

97

30.
___

The sons' lot the same as
their fathers', same faces

standing, waiting on the sidewalk.
Time will befall them in cars,
in removing and returning
Torah scrolls, in the cypress' wind.

Qassam rockets will roar as they migrate
north. Spring reflected
in scum upon the water,
in tar,
wax

suddenly the skin is furrowed,
dwindled like nakedness
the sex,
where was it, the street has taken away, taken where,
curse and awe

weighed down their tongues like
coins.

‎ל.

לַבָּנִים אוֹתוֹ גּוֹרָל כְּמוֹ
לָאָבוֹת, אוֹתָם פָּנִים

עוֹמְדִים וּמְחַכִּים עַל מִדְרָכָה.
הַזְּמַן יְקָרֶה לָהֶם בִּמְכוֹנִיּוֹת,
בְּהַכְנָסָה וְהוֹצָאַת סִפְרֵי
תּוֹרָה, בְּרוּחַ בַּבְּרוֹשִׁים.

קְסָאמִים יֶהֱמוּ בִּנְדִידָתָם אֶל
הַצָּפוֹן. אָבִיב דּוֹלֵק
בִּירוֹקָה עַל פְּנֵי הַמַּיִם,
בְּזֶפֶת,
שַׁעֲוָה

פִּתְאוֹם הָעוֹר חָרוּשׁ, הַמִּין דָּלִיל
כְּמוֹ עֶרְוָה,
אֵיפֹה הָיָה, הָרְחוֹב לָקַח לְאָן לָקַח,
קְלָלָה וְתַדְהֵמָה

כָּבְדוּ עַל לְשׁוֹנָם כְּמוֹ
מַטְבְּעוֹת.

31.

(Who would we have been if not dispersed, people

who don't ponder their collapse, in the synagogue always at home, fluent

in their language, rolled up in a purified body,

become one with it, who go home to find it there.

No, no going back, there's no return—

concrete existence.

No, it is not time that's crushed between the fingers, the burden of the lands of *Rephaim*;

nor poignant sweetness—a fist's distance parting earth and sky,

Adar crouches on the lawn like law, scarlet pimpernels

stripped bare, the promised rain is dammed

over the neem trees, charging up their growth.

In the streets adolescents pass in a daze,

and when the bombs grow silent

a group of *Bnei Akiva* craze

like Palestinians

on their

roof.)

לא.

(אִלְמָלֵא נִפְצוּנוּ מִי הָיִינוּ, אֲנָשִׁים
שֶׁלֹּא תוֹהִים עַל נִפּוּצָם. בְּבֵית הַכְּנֶסֶת לֹא חוֹרְגִים, יוֹדְעִים
אֶת הַשָּׂפָה, גְּלוּלִים בַּגּוּף הַמַּחְטָא
מִגַּלְגְּלִים אֵלַי, חוֹזְרִים הַבַּיְתָה וְיֵשְׁנוּ.
לֹא, לֹא חוֹזְרִים, אֵין חֲזָרָה -
קִיּוּם מַמָּשׁ.

לֹא זְמַן נִפְרָךְ בָּאֶצְבָּעוֹת, מַשָּׂא אַרְצוֹת הָרְפָאִים; לֹא נֹעַם
עַז - מֶרְחַק אֶגְרוֹף בֵּין הַשָּׁמַיִם לָרִצְפָה, אֲדַר רוֹבֵץ
עַל דְּשָׁאִים כְּמוֹ דִין, מַרְגָּנִיּוֹת קְרוּחוֹת, הַגֶּשֶׁם
הַמֻּבְטָח סָכוּר מֵעַל אִזְדָּרְכוֹת, טוֹעֵן אֶת
צְמִיחָתָן. בָּרְחוֹבוֹת הַנְּעוּרִים נָעִים,
שׁוּרָה שֶׁל בְּנֵי עֲקִיבָא בְּשַׁגַּם
בְּשֶׁךְ קַסָּאמִים מְרַקְדִים
כִּפְלַסְטִינִים עַל
גַּגָּם.)

32.

So where is the gate

in Gaza,

in Sderot—

The underworld of former times; the air

still faint

and we go through.

לב.

אָז הֵיכָן הוּא הַשַּׁעַר
בְּעַזָּה,
בִּשְׂדֵרוֹת -

עוֹלָם הַמֵּתִים שֶׁל פַּעַם; הָאֲוִיר
עוֹד דַּק
וַאֲנַחְנוּ עוֹבְרִים.

33.

For years I had this somber velvet
plunged between myself and forces shifting in the dark.

trapped within the synagogue till noon, vein-igniting purity,
then stepping out into the yard, an imposing ficus reigns

in stores of shade, among the foliage,
celestial voices chirp

in the thicket animals pass by, in the gaps
between the shuttered walls, three walls.

At dusk, when Sabbath ended,
my sister would bequeath me books, with fervent soul

I followed, little Sherlock Holmeses
run around with razored minds, slicing

piece by piece. For them, the body's devastation
is a departure point, a reason to entwine, to meld

the loved one's endlessness
into one deduction, all those branchings-out

שָׁנִים הָיְתָה לִי הַקְּטִיפָה הַזֹּו, כֵּהָה,
צְנוּחָה בֵּינִי וּבֵין כּוֹחוֹת זָעִים בַּחֹשֶׁךְ.

בְּבֵית הַכְּנֶסֶת סָגוּף עַד צָהֳרַיִם, טֹהַר מְלַקֵּחַ עוֹרְקִים,
וְאָז יוֹצֵא אֶל הֶחָצֵר, פִּיקוּס אֵימְתָנִי חוֹלֵשׁ

בְּמִגְּרוֹת שֶׁל צֵל, בֵּינוֹת לַעֲפָאִים
מִשְׂרְבָּבוֹת בְּנוֹת קוֹל, מְצַפְצְפוֹת

בְּתוֹךְ הַסְּבַךְ חוֹלְפוֹת חַיּוֹת, בְּרְוָחִים
בֵּין הַחוֹמוֹת הַמּוּגָפוֹת, שָׁלוֹשׁ חוֹמוֹת.

בָּעֲרָבִים, בְּצֵאת הַשַּׁבָּתוֹת צֻוְּתָה לִי
אֲחוֹתִי סְפָרִים, בְּנֶפֶשׁ מְאַמָּץ

אֲנִי עוֹקֵב, הַשֶּׁרְלוֹק הוֹלְמְסִים הַקְּטַנִּים
מִתְרוֹצְצִים עִם שֵׂכֶל מְתֹעָר, חוֹתְכִים

דָּבָר דָּבָר. לָהֶם כִּלְיוֹן הַגּוּף הוּא נְקֻדַּת
מוֹצָא, סִבָּה לִמְשֹׁךְ יַחְדָּו, לִמְסֹךְ

אֶת אֵינְסוֹפוֹ שֶׁל הָאָהוּב
לְתוֹךְ הֶקֵּשׁ אֶחָד, אֶת כָּל הַהִתְפָּרְדוּת

into one event, the smallest of the deeds,

sleep and awakenings, the incense of routine, a gaze

not wholly solved and thus awaits opaque

for resolution, kissed or untouched lips, spells

still singe their rims and the head trembles with bliss. And they were

right: God, death, a machine on space's border

were placed in ashen skies, the legions

of the stars above also followed with their eyes;

As for me, I did not notice their hum, or the flicker, or the drum

of the light's horses who hasten as they summon

the messengers, the pile of evidence—

the darkness beaten over Gaza, chiseled

pipes, gunpowder packed,

Tearing down the veil Sderot.

לְהִתְרַחֲשׁוּת, גּוֹנֵי גּוֹנָם שֶׁל מַעֲשִׂים,
שֵׁנָה וִיקִיצוֹת, קְטֹרֶת הַיּוֹמְיוֹם, מַבָּט

שֶׁלֹּא פָּעַנַח עַד תֹּם וְהוּא מַמְתִּין אָטוּם
לְגִלּוּיוֹ, שְׂפָתַיִם שֶׁנִּשְּׁקוּ אוֹ לֹא נָגְעוּ, לַחַשׁ

עוֹד חוֹרֵךְ אֶת שׁוּלֵיהֶן וְרֹאשׁ רוֹטֵט חֶמְדָּה. וּבֶאֱמֶת
צָדְקוּ: אֱלֹהִים, מָוֶת, מְכוֹנָה עַל גְּבוּל חִיצוֹן

הֻנְּחוּ בְּתוֹךְ שְׂחָקִים מַאֲפִירִים, גַּם לְגִיּוֹנוֹת
הַמְּאוֹרוֹת בָּלְשׁוּ מִתּוֹךְ חֲרִים;

לֵב לֹא נָתַתִּי אֲנִי לְזִמְזוּמָם, וְלָרְצוֹד, לְנְקִישַׁת
סוּסֵי הַנְּהָרָה הַמַּחִישִׁים בַּהֲחִישָׁם

אֶת הַשְּׁלִיחִים, אֶת עֲרֵמַת הָרְאָיוֹת –
הָעֲלָטָה הַחֲבוּטָה עַל עַזָּה, הַצִּנּוֹרוֹת

הַחֲרוּטִים, דְּחוּסִים אֲבַק שְׂרֵפָה,
פּוֹרְמִים אֶת הַפַּרְגּוֹד שֶׁדֵּרוֹת.

34.

In the year nineteen eighty-seven
I thought the end of the world
was near,
with the sun opaque as the gaze
of a porn star (what was it—
the pleasure? the apathy of heroin?) and summer,
in my memories, eternal
summer

they aired a reality
show: who wants
to plunge down into
the ruse of electricity, the sapphires,
the sharp ice anointed into shapes

and the American, the conqueror of moons,
fixed his binoculars on me, a painful lens,
the neighborhood's cars
howled, birds on the run,
the blind seraph in Sderot's intersection
spewed out: what's wrong with you lately

לד.

בִּשְׁנַת אֶלֶף תְּשַׁע מֵאוֹת שְׁמוֹנִים וְשֶׁבַע
חָשַׁבְתִּי שֶׁסּוֹף הָעוֹלָם
כְּבָר קָרוֹב,
עִם שֶׁמֶשׁ אָטוֹם כְּמוֹ מַבָּט
שֶׁל כּוֹכֶבֶת פּוֹרְנוֹ (מָה הָיָה זֶה –
הָעֹנֶג? קֵהוּת הָרוֹאִין?) וְקַיִץ,
בְּזִכְרוֹנוֹתַי קַיִץ
תָּמִיד

בַּטֶּלֶוִיזְיָה שֶׁדָּרָה
תָּכְנִית מְצִיאוּת: מִי רוֹצֶה
לָרֶדֶת אֶל בֵּין
תַּחְבּוּלוֹת הַחַשְׁמַל, סַפִּירִים,
קֶרַח חַד חָבוּר כְּמָשִׁיחָה

וְהָאָמֶרִיקָאִי כּוֹבֵשׁ הַיְּרֵחִים
לָטַשׁ בִּי מִשְׁקֶפֶת, עֲדָשָׁה מַכְאִיבָה,
רִכְבֵי הַשְּׁכוּנָה
יִלְלוּ, צִפּוֹרִים אֲנוּסוֹת,
הַשָּׂרָף הָעֵר שֶׁבְּצַמֶּת שְׂדֵרוֹת
רֶשֶׁף מָה אַתָּה, בַּזְּמַן הָאַחֲרוֹן

you're never home when I call

a lovely curse lay on my lips
and my father clawed my tongue
but dad, I said,
being who I am,
human and limited and mortal,
any attribute of grace is lacking
from my body
in the year of nineteen eighty-seven

and the halt is so quick to arrive.

אַתָּה אַף פַּעַם לֹא בַּבַּיִת
כְּשֶׁאֲנִי מִתְקַשֵּׁר

קִטְרוּג יְפַהְפֶּה הֻנַּח עַל שְׂפָתַי
וְאָבִי אָחַז בְּצֶבֶת לְשׁוֹנִי,
אֲבָל אַבָּא, אָמַרְתִּי,
מֵעֶצֶם מִי שֶׁאֲנִי
אֱנוֹשִׁי וּמְגֻבָּל וּבֶן מָוֶת
כָּל מִדָּה שֶׁל חֶסֶד נְטוּלָה
מִגּוּפִי
בִּשְׁנַת אֶלֶף תְּשַׁע מֵאוֹת שְׁמוֹנִים וְשֶׁבַע

וְהַדָּם מְמַהֵר כֹּה לָבוֹא.

35.

Pillars of thistle in the storm's electric bright
only thus might I capture
Adar

A body pierced by fine pins, flame
falling from the heavens, touch anchored
in the void

Friday's dusk, between the days,
will finally be settled
guilt made of guilt

לה.

עַמּוּדֵי בְּרָקָן בְּחַשְׁמַל הַסּוּפָה
רַק כָּךְ אֶפְשָׁר שֶׁאָצוּד אֶת
אֲדָר

גּוּף נָקוּב בְּחֲדִים, לַהַט
מָט מֵרְקִיעִים, הַמַּגָּע הֶעָגוּן
עַל בְּלִימָה

יוֹם שִׁשִּׁי בֵּין שְׁמָשׁוֹת
יֵרָשֵׁם לְבַסּוֹף
אַשְׁמָה עֲשׂוּיָה בְּאַשְׁמָה

36.

For one day I will desert that city-far-off,

that needle-like pleasure, that desert.

If only nerves of daylight would dart into the heavens' vault

like wounds budding from a wasp's sting

on the day I depart from far-off

to make out of myself a man

who I will fail, time and again,

to make my own.

17.

כִּי יוֹם אֶחָד אֲנִי עוֹרֵק מֵעִיר-שַׁמָּה,
מִתַּעֲנוּג עַרְעַר, מֵעֲרָבָה.
לוּ יַעַמְדוּ בָּרְקִיעִים עַצַּבֵּי שֶׁמֶשׁ
כַּעֲפָצִים עוֹלִים מֵעֲקִיצַת צִרְעָה
בַּיּוֹם הַזֶּה שֶׁבּוֹ אֲנִי עוֹזֵב אֶת שָׁם
עוֹשֶׂה עַצְמִי אָדָם
שֶׁכָּל חַיַּי יִקְשֶׁה לִי
לְנָשְׁמוֹ.

37.

Sex and loneliness and coals

stars of coal,

black cries, the economy of crows,

speckling them with holes.

The nail in the hand, the nail in the head,

the wreckage of darkness and teeth marks of words.

In the morning, once more, I did not know what should be done with the blood—

it moves from me to the world in a flood.

לז.

מִין וּבְדִידוּת וּפֶחָם,
כּוֹכָבִים שֶׁל פֶּחָם,
זְעָקוֹת שְׁחֹרוֹת, כַּלְכָּלַת הָעוֹרְבִים
הַנּוֹקְרִים בְּתוֹכָם.

הַמַּסְמֵר שֶׁבַּיָּד, הַמַּסְמֵר שֶׁבָּרֹאשׁ,
שֶׁבֶר הַחֹשֶׁךְ וּנְשִׁיכַת הַמִּלָּה.
בַּבֹּקֶר שׁוּב לֹא יָדַעְתִּי מָה יֵעָשֶׂה עִם הַדָּם -
זֶה עוֹזֵב אוֹתִי וְהוֹלֵךְ לָעוֹלָם.

38.

Like lovers who house-warmed by fucking
in every corner, madness
thrust against the walls, on the counter, trapped
in kitchen drawers,
I too cried for Tel Aviv:

This saltiness will not swerve
from the ficus trees, from these skies
enrobing themselves in *Tevet* like a young nude
exposed in mid-shower.

And the smell of tearing flesh
will cling to the sidewalks, to the climbing prices
of apartments, to those beasts on their bicycles
sparing themselves on the seashore,

to the relentless pulse
of wireless transmission.
Your whitened blood will shoot its arrow—
And I'll deliver into ruin that city of extremes
hater of the poor, of the lonely,
of the pursuer of
dreams.

לח.

כָּאוֹהֲבִים אֲשֶׁר חָנְכוּ בֵּיתָם בְּזִיּוּנִים
בְּכָל פִּנָּה, פְּרָאוּת
מוּטַחַת בַּכְּתָלִים, בַּשַּׁיִשׁ, תְּפוּסָה בְּמִגְרוֹת
מִטְבָּח,
בָּכִיתִי גַם אֲנִי אֶת תֵּל אָבִיב:

מְלִיחוּת זוֹ לֹא תָסוּר
מֵעַם הַפִּיקוּסִים, מִן הַשְּׁחָקִים
הַמִּתְכַּסִּים טֶבַח כְּנַעֲרָה
שֶׁהִתְפָּרְצוּ אֶל מִקְלַחְתָּהּ.

וְרֵיחַ הַקְּרָעוֹת בָּשָׂר
יִדְבַּק בַּמִּדְרָכוֹת, בִּמְחִירֵי דִּירוֹת
מַאֲמִירִים, בַּבְּהֵמוֹת הַנּוֹשְׁעִים
בְּאוֹפַנֵּיהֶם עַל קַו הַחוֹף,

בָּהֲלֹם
הַנָּחוּשׁ שֶׁל תִּמְסוֹרוֹת אַלְחוּטִיּוֹת.
דָּמֵךְ שֶׁהִיא הַלְּבִינָה שׁוֹט יַקְשָׁט -
מָסַרְתִּי לְחָרְבָּה אֶת הַקִּרְיָה הַזֹּאת
שׂוֹנֵאת לָעֲנִיִּים, לַגַּלְמוּדִים,
לְבַעֲלֵי
הַחֲלוֹמוֹת.

39.

Sderot is clenched in winter, a radiance of cotton caresses

from above. First the warblers

stiffen to fall,

then bushes glazed with ice

crop up, a whack, chime rings against

the winds, then the engines spin

and rasp, a swish blows past, it is the cypress trees, I think,

flap and flutter, crows laden with moans

across a streetlight. And your voice arrives, no longer lost

in music, no longer sweetened—as from now on

it shall ring, as it had always rung, it is I

who hears its crack

I whose life has been a detour

from your

lack.

לט.

שְׂדֵרוֹת נִקְפֶּצֶת חֹרֶף, קִרְיַת כַּתְנָה נוֹשֶׁקֶת
מַרְקִיעִים. תְּחִלָּה הַפְּשׁוֹשִׁים
קְשׁוּיִים לַנְּפִילָה,
אַחַר כָּךְ מִתְגַּשְּׁמִים
שִׂיחִים מִזְּגָגֵי קָרָה, מַכָּה, דִּנְדוּן כְּנֶגֶד
הָרוּחוֹת, וְאָז הַמְּנוֹעִים סַבִּים
וְנַחֲרִים, וְיֵשׁ וְשַׁוְּשׁ, נִדְמֶה לִי שֶׁבְּרֹאשִׁים
טְפִיחוֹת, טְפִיחוֹת, טְפִיחוֹת, עוֹרְבִים כְּבֵדִים כַּאֲנָחוֹת
עַל פְּנֵי רְחוֹב. וּבָא קוֹלְךָ, לֹא עוֹד אוֹבֵד
בַּנְּגִינָה, לֹא עוֹד נִמְתָּק – כְּפִי
שֶׁיִּהְיֶה מִכָּאן, כְּפִי שֶׁתָּמִיד הִנּוֹ, אֲנִי
הוּא הַשּׁוֹמֵעַ
שֶׁכָּל חַיַּי עַד כָּאן
הָיוּ הֶסַּח שֶׁלֹּא
אֶתְגַּעֲגֵעַ.

40.

I'll probably lose my mind, this dick just doesn't hold

memory oddity identity. Everyone knows to babble something or another

about the fraying, the stutter, as if the GodofDeath

had not yet emerged and were a polished blade, a praising sound of the *Shofar*, behold and you too shall

see, He will leave you nothing but a crevice in the throat through which I

whisper to my sister: take thee a portion of my body that you may live. And to Tel Aviv,

to her I sing afresh: youth bathed in flesh, newspapers soaring on

the city's curse, trade thieving your past and your trees – what have I to do with your Glory

and you with your deeds. It just doesn't hold. And to Sderot I'm thrust

on a chariot of fire to ask the pardon of Tamar, my mother, oh mother, countless times it will befall her,

she will raise her voice and weep, like a maniac I'm running up and down the streets, I'm leaving home

only for the graveyard. And brothers and sisters and nephews and nieces, don't think oh

so hearty, this familial warmth and the simplicity of being. There's only a preachy *Drash* side to this

story, your loved ones make demands, on end, grab you by the hand, you cross the river there

you'll forget, Amen I say, say to whom, why did you allow the miracles to grind your bones

in a decelerated crash. Draining calcium, fractures not yet healed, eroded joints,

it's time, eventually you will adapt to time, your expiration date has passed, mammals flirting on the

estuary of history. Like that sight of boundless splendor I've envisioned in a dream, driving

in an AIL Storm collapsed of its troops, Aviva at my side, in the distance a white tower shouts at the

clouds, *Mitzpe Ramon* I conjecture in her ear, we're heading to Eilat, but no desert is in view, *Kurkar*

sandstones and open lakes resting in their sockets, glinting fish, fowl perhaps, gaped

hibiscus groaning, braying: wake. And I arouse to a morning of ecstatic light.

מ.

קָרוֹב לְוַדַּאי שֶׁאֶשְׁתַּגֵּעַ, לֹא מַחְזִיק הַזִּיו הַזֶּה

זְרוֹת זְכָרוֹת זֵהוּת. כֻּלָּם יוֹדְעִים לְבַרְבֵּר מַשֶּׁהוּ אֶחָד

עַל הַפְּרָמִים, עַל הַגִּמְגּוּם, כְּאִלּוּ אֱלֹהִימוּת

לֹא הִגִּיחַ וְהוּא לַהַב מְמֹרָט, הוּא תֶּקַע שׁוֹפָר, רָאֹה תִּרְאוּ כָּמוֹנִי הוּא יַשְׁאִיר לָכֶם

רַק סֶדֶק בַּגָּרוֹן שֶׁבַּעֲדוֹ אֲנִי

לוֹאֵט אֶל אֲחוֹתִי: קְחִי לָךְ הַחֵלֶק מִגּוּפִי וַחֲיִי מִמֶּנּוּ לְמַעַן תִּחְיִי. וְלָתֵל אָבִיב

לָהּ אֲנִי שָׁר: הַנְּעוּרִים הַנִּרְחָצִים בָּשָׂר, הָעִתּוֹנִים הַמַּגְבִּיהֵיהֶם אֲוִיר עַל

תֵּאַלַת הָעִיר, הַמִּסְחָר הַמְּגֻנֶּב אֶת עֲבָרֵךְ וְאֶת עֲצִיֵךְ – לָמָה לִי תְּהִלָּתֵךְ

וְלָמָה לָךְ יָמַיִךְ. זֶה לֹא מַחְזִיק. וְלִשְׂדֵרוֹת אֲנִי נִדְחָף

בְּרֶכֶב אֵשׁ לְחַלּוֹת פְּנֵי תָּמָר, אִמִּי, אִמִּי, אֵינְסְפוֹר פְּעָמִים יְקָרָה לָהּ,

הִיא תֵּבֵךְ, אֲנִי יָרוּץ כְּמוֹ מְטֹרֶפֶת בָּרְחוֹבוֹת, מֵהַבַּיִת אֲנִי

יָצֹא רַק לְבֵית הָעָלְמִין. וְאַחִים וַאֲחָיוֹת וְאַחְיָנִים אַחְיָנִיּוֹת, אַל תַּחְשְׁבוּ כַּמָּה חָמִים, אָה,

הַחֲמִימוּת הַמִּשְׁפַּחְתִּית הַזֹּאת, וּפְשְׁטוּתוֹ שֶׁל הַקִּיּוּם. רַק דְּרָשׁ יֵשׁ בַּסִּפּוּר, אֲהוּבֵיכֶם דּוֹרְשִׁים

אֶתְכֶם, קַו לָקָו, לוֹקְחִים אֶתְכֶם בַּיָּד, אַתֶּם חוֹצִים אֶת הַנָּהָר שָׁם

תִּשְׁכְּחוּ, אָמֵן אֲנִי אוֹמֵר לָכֶם, לְמִי אֲנִי אוֹמֵר, לָמָה הִנַּחְתֶּם לַנָּסִים לִמְחֹץ עַצְמוֹתֵיכֶם

בְּהִתְרַסְּקוּת מוּאֶטֶת. סִידָן דּוֹלֵף, שֶׁבָרִים שֶׁלֹּא הֶחְלִימוּ עַד תֻּמָּם, שְׁחוּקִים הַמִּפְרָקִים,

הִגִּיעַ זְמַן, לַזְמַן כְּבָר תִּתְרַגְּלוּ, כְּבָר נִפְגַּחְתֶּם, יוֹנְקִים עוֹגְבִים עַל

שֶׁפֶךְ הַהִיסְטוֹרְיָה. כַּמַּחֲזֶה אֲשֶׁר חָזִיתִי יְפִי בַחֲלוֹם לֹא אֵין שִׁעוּר לוֹ, נוֹהֵג בְּתוֹךְ סוּפָה

הַמִּתְכַּלָּה מֵחֲלַיָתָה, אֲבִיבָה לְצִדִּי, בַּמֶּרְחַקִּים מִגְדָּל לָבָן צָעוּק אֶל עֲנָנִים, מִצְפֶּה רָמוֹן

שַׁעֲרִיתִי בְּאָזְנָה, אֲנַחְנוּ בַּדֶּרֶךְ לְאֵילַת, וְאֵין מִדְבָּר, צְבִירֵי כָּרָךְ וַאֲגַמִּים פְּתוּחִים

בִּשְׁקִעֵיהֶם, דָּגִים מְבַהֲקִים, סָפֵק עוֹפוֹת, הִיבִּיסְקוּסִים פְּעוּרֵי

לָעוֹת מְנַאֲקִים וְנוֹעֲרִים לִי עוֹד. אֲנִי נֵעוֹר אֶל בֹּקֶר מֻרְגָּשׁ מֵאוֹר.

One can claim eternity is this, I told my mother

and she replied, both of us caught in the congealment of all brightness, we did not utter her name

lest we burst, just like at nights when my mind turns to glass, on the verge of pounding

against the skull. But of factories destroyed by barren shooting we spoke. We pawned

another hour of ourselves in that way, Amen I tell you, this is the secret, to linger is the

essence of it all, like the emergency alert system hindering with a strident murmur

the movement of bombs alive with fire.

אֶפְשָׁר לִטְעֹן שֶׁזֶּה הַנֶּצַח, אָמַרְתִּי לְאִמִּי
וְהִיא עָנְתָה, שְׁרוּיִים בְּהִתְקָרְשׁוּת הַזֹּהַר בָּעוֹלָם, אֶת שְׁמָה לֹא הֶעֱלִינוּ פֶּן
נִפְרֹץ, כְּמוֹ בָּעֲרָבִים שֶׁאָז מוֹחִי זְכוּכִית, נִדְמֶה שֶׁהִנֵּה הוּא נִדְפָּק
כְּנֶגֶד הַגֻּלְגֹּלֶת. אֲבָל עַל הֶרֶס מִפְעָלִים מִיְּדֵי רֵיק דִּבַּרְנוּ. מִשֶּׁכַּנּוּ עוֹד שָׁעָה
אֶצְלֵנוּ, אָמֵן אֲנִי אוֹמֵר לָכֶם, שֶׁזֶּה הַסּוֹד, מַהוּת הַכֹּל הִתְמַהְמְהוּת, כְּהִסָּחוֹסָהּ שֶׁל
מַעֲרֶכֶת הַכְּרִיזָה הַמְעַכֶּבֶת בְּגִרְגּוּר צוֹרֵם רָקָטוֹת לוֹהֲבוֹת.

41.

Orchid, a tree, perhaps

only a bush, and still, a verdant vessel

seizing voices that *Nissan*

threatens to eject: a stamen—a caw of color, a petal—

a howl of hue.

This is all in reach, that is,

unreachable, in Gaza, in Sderot,

an enthralled *Adar* is swarming. Heavy mud,

fowl of all kinds wrack houses with their squalls,

a moon, the heart of day, pillars of dust.

This is all in reach, that is, retracted

from the world, detached from me—

Is this the journey's end?

I am bewildered,

still none the wiser—

And if this is its cusp,

weary as I am, how will I begin

מא.

בּוֹהִינְיָה, עֵץ, אוּלַי

רַק שִׂיחַ, בְּכָל זֹאת, בָּזֶיךְ יָרֹק

כֻּלֹּא קוֹלוֹת אֲשֶׁר נִיסָן גּוֹהֵר

לִפְרֹץ: אַבְקָן – צְנִיפָה שֶׁל צֶבַע, עָלֶה כּוֹתֶרֶת –

בְּכִי גָוֶן.

כָּל זֶה מְשָׁג, מַשְׁמָע,

בִּלְתִּי מְשָׁג, בְּעַזָּה, בִּשְׂדֵרוֹת

רוֹחֵשׁ אֲדַר אֶלֶף. בֵּ׳ן כָּבֵד,

מִינֵי עוֹפוֹת הוֹרְסִים בָּתִּים בְּצַוְּחָתָם,

יָרֵחַ, לֵב הַיּוֹם, תִּימֹרֶת שֶׁל אָבָק.

כָּל זֶה מְשָׁג, מַשְׁמָע מוּסָג מִן

הָעוֹלָם, נִפְרָד מִמֶּנִּי –

הֲזֶה סוֹפוֹ שֶׁל הַמַּסָּע?

אֲנִי מֻפְתָּע

לֹא הֶחְכַּמְתִּי -

וְאִם סָפוֹ,

אֲנִי עָיֵף, כֵּיצַד אַתְחִיל

42.

This poem is not fit for music, it reaches from afar,
from a kingdom where no tune is needed.
There's no breaking through from there to darkness
to single handedly recover the shards—

only ghosts once flesh and voice

and the worldly land laden with roads
Sderot-Tel Aviv, Gaza-Sderot, a magnetized
snap on a Strip of tape:

sighs of song in cities pressed by deimos at sundown, an eyeball
slashed as it sees, the possibility is a blade, a little gleaming blade,
Majbed, shidi al ha-shba, sahadi be-za'in
He ridicules from His heavens—
to get up from the shiv'ah on "And Jacob dwelt"
visit the gravesite on "And Jacob lived"

Climb and shake the trees to learn,
do the waters have names? And savor, not an ashen
sting, and go hold sway over the fowl of the air
and every living thing that moves upon the earth,
over that called fire, for example, what heat did you discover there?

מב.

וּמוּסִיקָה לַשִּׁיר הַזֶּה אֵין, מֵרָחוֹק הוּא מַגִּיעַ,
מַמְלָכוּת אֵין לָהּ צֹרֶךְ בִּצְלִיל.
לֹא הוֹרְסִים מִשָּׁם אֶל הַחֹשֶׁךְ
לְהָשִׁיב בְּיָד חֲרָסִים –

רַק רְפָאוֹת שֶׁהָיְתָה בָּשָׂר וְקוֹלוֹת

וְהָאָרֶץ אַרְצִית חֲרוּצָה בְּצִירִים
שְׂדֵרוֹת־תֵּל אָבִיב, עַזָּה־שְׂדֵרוֹת, פִּצְפוּן
מְמֻגְנָט בִּרְצוּעַת הַקְלָטָה:

רַחַשׁ עֲנוּת, בֶּעָרִים מְעוּכוֹת דִּימוֹסֵי הַזְּרִיחָה, גַּלְגַּל עַיִן
שֶׁסַּף בִּשְׁעַת רְאִיָּה, אֶפְשָׁרוּת הִיא לַהַב, לַהַב קָטָן וְנוֹצֵץ,
מִזְ׳בֵּד, שִׁדֵּי עַל הַשִּׁבָּה, סַחֲדֵי בְּזַיִן
רְקִיעָיו צְחוֹק עָשָׂה –
לְשֶׁבֶת מִן הָאֵבֶל פָּרָשַׁת וַיֵּשֶׁב
לַעֲלוֹת אֶל הַקֶּבֶר פָּרָשַׁת וַיְחִי.

זַעְזְעוּ וְטִפְּסוּ בָּעֵצִים וְגָלוּ,
יֵשׁ לַמַּיִם שֵׁמוֹת? וְטַעַם, לֹא דַק
מֵעָפָר, וְרְדוּ לִרְדּוֹת בְּחַיַּת הַשָּׂדֶה וּבָעוֹף,
בְּזוּ הַקְּרוּיָה אֵשׁ, לְמָשָׁל, אֵיזֶה חֹם מְצָאתֶם?

Tell me, though night already offered up his lips

and a mighty moon is wrinkled

in his throat—

Ever since creation ceased, the dead have spoken

in Hebrew:

on 18 *Kislev 5768*,

only inches came between

the toilet seat

and the Seat of Mercy.

אָמְרוּ לִי, אַף שֶׁלַּיְלָה הִגִּישׁ אֶת שְׂפָתָיו
וּלְבָנָה אַדִּירָה קְמוּטָה
בִּגְרוֹנוֹ –

מִיּוֹם שֶׁחָדְלָה הַבְּרִיאָה, דִּבְּרוּ הַמֵּתִים
בְּעִבְרִית:
יוֹד חֵית בְּכִסְלֵו הַתַּשְׁסַח
סַנְטִים מַחְרִיד
אֶת בֵּית הַכִּסֵּא
מִכִּסֵּא הַכָּבוֹד.

43.

A psalm for Tamar may you be saved from the ashes

from ashen days and ashen dust

and if in this life there is a life beyond the life of the body

may you have it

and may you be kept from the temptation to hover once again with him, the drunkard

your heart for his heart, your tongue for his tongue

before the first word is uttered

Sderot, Tel Aviv Jaffa

25 Kislev – Rosh Chodesh Adar II, 5768

מג.

מִזְמוֹר לְתָמָר יוֹשִׁיעוּךְ מִן הָאֵפֶר
מִיָּמִים שֶׁל אֵפֶר מִן הָאֵפֶר גַּם
וְאִם יֵשׁ בְּחַיִּים אֵלֶּה חַיִּים מֵעֵבֶר לְחַיֵּי הַגּוּף
יִתְּנוּךְ אוֹתָם
וְיִשְׁמְרוּךְ מִן הַפִּתּוּי לָשׁוּב אֶל הָרְחִיפָה אִתּוֹ־שִׁכּוֹר
לְבֵּךְ תַּחַת לִבּוֹ שְׂפָתָיו תַּחַת שְׂפָתֵךְ
בְּטֶרֶם תֵּאָמֵר הַמִּלָּה הָרִאשׁוֹנָה

שדרות, תל אביב יפו
כ"ה כסלו – ר"ח אדר ב', התשס"ח

135

Recent Titles from Alice James Books

Half/Life: New & Selected Poems, Jeffrey Thomson

Odes to Lithium, Shira Erlichman

Here All Night, Jill McDonough

To the Wren: Collected & New Poems, Jane Mead

Angel Bones, Ilyse Kusnetz

Monsters I Have Been, Kenji C. Liu

Soft Science, Franny Choi

Bicycle in a Ransacked City: An Elegy, Andrés Cerpa

Anaphora, Kevin Goodan

Ghost, like a Place, Iain Haley Pollock

Isako Isako, Mia Ayumi Malhotra

Of Marriage, Nicole Cooley

The English Boat, Donald Revell

We, the Almighty Fires, Anna Rose Welch

DiVida, Monica A. Hand

pray me stay eager, Ellen Doré Watson

Some Say the Lark, Jennifer Chang

Calling a Wolf a Wolf, Kaveh Akbar

We're On: A June Jordan Reader, Edited by Christoph Keller and Jan Heller Levi

Daylily Called It a Dangerous Moment, Alessandra Lynch

Surgical Wing, Kristin Robertson

The Blessing of Dark Water, Elizabeth Lyons

Reaper, Jill McDonough

Madwoman, Shara McCallum

Contradictions in the Design, Matthew Olzmann

House of Water, Matthew Nienow

World of Made and Unmade, Jane Mead

Driving without a License, Janine Joseph

The Big Book of Exit Strategies, Jamaal May

play dead, francine j. harris

Thief in the Interior, Phillip B. Williams

Second Empire, Richie Hofmann

Drought-Adapted Vine, Donald Revell

Refuge/es, Michael Broek

O'Nights, Cecily Parks

Alice James Books is committed to publishing books that matter. The press was founded in 1973 in Boston, Massachusetts as a cooperative, wherein authors performed the day-to-day undertakings of the press. This element remains present today, as authors who publish with the press are invited to collaborate closely in the publication process of their work. AJB remains committed to its founders' original feminist mission, while expanding upon the scope to include all voices and poets who might otherwise go unheard. In keeping with its efforts to build equity and increase inclusivity in publishing and the literary arts, AJB seeks out poets whose writing possesses the range, depth, and ability to cultivate empathy in our world and to dynamically push against silence. The press was named for Alice James, sister to William and Henry, whose extraordinary gift for writing went unrecognized during her lifetime.

Designed by Tiani Kennedy

Printed by McNaughton & Gunn